Algebra 1

Practice Workbook

Houghton Mifflin Harcourt

ISBN   978-0-544-71632-2

2 3 4 5 6 7 8 9 10   0928   24 23 22 21 20 19

4500747074   B C D E F G

Contents

Student Worksheets

LESSON 1-1 Solving Equations

Practice and Problem Solving: A/B

Use the guess-and-check method to solve. Show your work.

1. $x + 8 = 11$

2. $5y - 9 = 16$

_____   _____

Solve by working backward. Show your work.

3. $x - 4 = 9$

4. $3y + 4 = 10$

_____   _____

Solve the equation by using the Properties of Equality.

5. $6c + 3 = 45$

6. $11 - a = -23$

_____   _____

7. $\dfrac{2}{3} + y = \dfrac{1}{4}$

8. $\dfrac{7}{8}w = 14$

_____   _____

Solve.

9. Houston, Texas has an average annual rainfall about 5.2 times that of El Paso, Texas. If Houston gets about 46 inches of rain, about how many inches does El Paso get? Round to the nearest tenth.

_____

10. Susan can run 2 city blocks per minute. She wants to run 60 blocks. How long will it take her to finish if she has already run 18 blocks?

_____

11. Michaela pays her cell phone service provider $49.95 per month for 500 minutes. Any additional minutes used cost $0.15 each. In June, her phone bill is $61.20. How many additional minutes did she use?

_____

Solving Equations
Practice and Problem Solving: C

Use the guess-and-check method to solve. Show your work.

1. $26 = t - 19$

2. $w - 2 = -43$

_____

_____

Solve by working backward. Show your work.

3. $8n + 6 = 46$

4. $15 - 3y = -3$

_____

_____

Solve the equation by using the Properties of Equality.

5. $2(8 + k) = 22$

6. $m + 5(m - 1) = 7$

_____

_____

7. $-13 = 2b - b - 10$

8. $\dfrac{2}{3}x - \dfrac{5}{8}x = 26$

_____

_____

Solve.

9. Sam is moving into a new apartment. Before he moves in, the landlord asks that he pay the first month's rent and a security deposit equal to 1.5 times the monthly rent. The total that Sam pays the landlord before he moves in is $3275. What is the monthly rent?

_____

10. Mr. Rodriguez invests half his money in land, a tenth in stocks, and a twentieth in bonds. He puts the remaining $35,000 in his savings account. What is the total amount of money that Mr. Rodriguez saves and invests?

_____

11. A work crew has a new pump and an old pump. The new pump can fill a tank in 5 hours, and the old pump can fill the same tank in 7 hours. Write and solve an equation for the time it will take both pumps to fill one tank if the pumps are used together.

_____

LESSON
1-2
Modeling Quantities
Practice and Problem Solving: A/B

Use ratios to solve the problems.

The diagram below represents a tree and a mailbox and their shadows.
The heights of the triangles represent the heights of the objects, and the
longer sides represent their shadows.

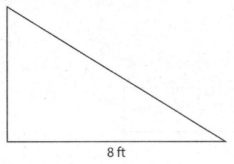
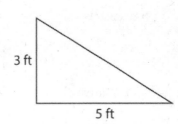

8 ft   3 ft   5 ft

1. What is the height of the tree? _____

Use the diagram below for 2–5.

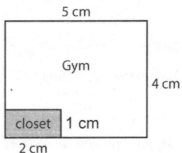

5 cm

Gym

4 cm

closet | 1 cm

2 cm

2. If 1 cm represents 10 m, what are the actual measurements of the gym

   including the closet? _____

3. What are the actual measurements of the closet? _____

4. If 1 cm represents 12 m, what are the actual measurements of the gym including the

   closet? _____

5. What is the area of the gym? _____

Solve.

Selena rides her bicycle to work. It takes her 15 minutes to go 3 miles.

6. If she continues at the same rate, how long will it take her to go 8 miles?

   _____

7. How many feet will she travel in 3 minutes?

   _____

LESSON 1-2

Modeling Quantities

Practice and Problem Solving: C

Use a ruler to measure the distance to solve.

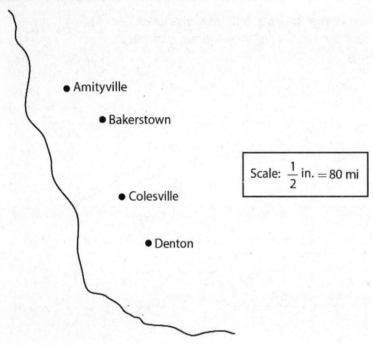

Scale: $\frac{1}{2}$ in. = 80 mi

1. What is the distance between Bakerstown and Denton?

   _____

2. What is the distance between Bakerstown and Colesville?

   _____

3. If Sarah drives 55 miles per hour, how long will it take her to drive from Amityville to Denton?

   _____

4. Hector drives 60 miles an hour from Amityville to Eaglecroft. If it takes him 5 hours and 45 minutes, what is the distance between the two cities?

   _____

5. If the scale of the map changes, and the new distance between Amityville and Denton is 325 miles, what is the new scale?

   _____

Name _____ Date _____ Class_____

Reporting with Precision and Accuracy
Practice and Problem Solving: A/B

Identify the more precise measurement.

1. 16 ft; 6 in.

2. 4.8 L; 2 mL

3. 4 pt; 1 gal

_____

_____

_____

4. 9.3 mg; 7.05 mg

5. 74 mm; 2.25 cm

6. 12 oz; 11 lb

_____

_____

_____

Find the number of significant digits in each example.

7. 52.9 km

8. 800 ft

9. 70.09 in.

_____

_____

_____

10. 0.6 mi

11. 23.0 g

12. 3120.58 m

_____

_____

_____

Order each list of units from most precise to least precise.

13. yard, inch, foot, mile

14. gram, centigram, kilogram, milligram

_____

_____

Rewrite each number with the number of significant digits indicated in parentheses.

15. 12.32 lb (2)

16. 1.8 m (1)

17. 34 mi (4)

_____

_____

_____

Solve.

18. A rectangular garden has length of 24 m and width of 17.2 m. Use the correct number of significant digits to write the perimeter of the garden.

_____

19. Kelly is making a beaded bracelet with beads that measure 4 mm and 7.5 mm long. If the bracelet is 15 cm long and Kelly uses the same number of each type bead, about how many beads will she use?

_____

20. When two people each measured a window's width, their results were 79 cm and 786 mm. Are these results equally precise? Explain.

_____

Name _____ Date _____ Class_____

 LESSON 1-3 # Reporting with Precision and Accuracy
Practice and Problem Solving: C

Choose the most precise measurement in each set.

1. 7.0 cm; 700 cm; 7000 cm   2. 30 cm; 30 m; 32 mm   3. 9.5 lb; 0.1 oz; 4 oz

_____   _____   _____

For each measurement, find the number of significant digits.

4. 800 kg   5. 20.0594 km   6. 0.0009 mm

_____   _____   _____

Rewrite each number with the number of significant digits indicated in parentheses.

7. 0.09 mL (2)   8. 5280 ft (1)   9. 9.006 g (3)

_____   _____   _____

Solve.

10. Explain how someone could say the following: "I used to think that 17 and 17.0 were the same. But now I am beginning to wonder."

_____

_____

11. As part of an experiment, a student combined 3.4 g of one chemical with 0.56 g of a second chemical. He then recorded the combined mass as 4 g. Did the student record the combined mass correctly? Explain.

_____

_____

12. Building lumber is labeled according to the dimensions (in inches) of its cross section. So, a "two-by-four" measures 2 inches by 4 inches, but not exactly. In fact, the cross section of a two-by-four has the smallest dimensions possible, while still legitimately being called a two-by-four. Find those dimensions. Then find the percent by which the cross-sectional area of a two-by-four is less than that of a "true" two-by-four.

_____

_____

_____

Name _____ Date _____ Class_____

 # Modeling with Expressions

Practice and Problem Solving: A/B

Identify the terms and coefficients of each expression.

1. $4a + 3c + 8$

   terms: _____

   coefficients: _____

2. $9b + 6 + 2g$

   terms: _____

   coefficients: _____

3. $8.1f + 15 + 2.7g$

   terms: _____

   coefficients: _____

4. $7p - 3r + 6 - 5s$

   terms: _____

   coefficients: _____

5. $3m - 2 - 5n + p$

   terms: _____

   coefficients: _____

6. $4.6w - 3 + 6.4x - 1.9y$

   terms: _____

   coefficients: _____

Interpret the meaning of the expression.

7. Frank buys p pounds of oranges for $2.29 per pound and the same number of pounds of apples for $1.69 per pound. What does the expression $2.29p + 1.69p$ represent?

   _____

8. Kathy buys p pounds of grapes for $2.19 per pound and one pound of kiwi for $3.09 per pound. What does the expression $2.19p - 3.09$ represent?

   _____

Write an expression to represent each situation.

9. Eliza earns $400 per week plus $15 for each new customer she signs up. Let c represent the number of new customers Eliza signs up. Write an expression that shows how much she earns in a week.

   _____

10. Max's car holds 18 gallons of gasoline. Driving on the highway, the car uses approximately 2 gallons per hour. Let h represent the number of hours Max has been driving on the highway. Write an expression that shows how many gallons of gasoline Max has left after driving h hours.

    _____

11. A man's age today is three years less than four times the age of his oldest daughter. Let a represent the daughter's age. Write an expression to represent the man's age.

    _____

LESSON 2-1

Modeling with Expressions

Practice and Problem Solving: C

Simplify each expression when you can. Then identify the terms and coefficients of each.

1. $5b + 6d - 5c + 19a$

   terms: _____

   coefficients: _____

2. $4w - 5 + 6(2x + 7) - 19$

   terms: _____

   coefficients: _____

3. $12 + 8r - 3(s - 5) + 15t$

   terms: _____

   coefficients: _____

4. $9g - 2(-h + 3j) + 7 - 8k$

   terms: _____

   coefficients: _____

Write a situation that could be represented by the expression.

5. $3a + 6$, where a = age in years

   _____

6. $5(p + 2)$, where p = the number of points scored

   _____

Write an expression for each situation. Then solve the problem.

7. A man's age today is 2 years more than three times the age his son will be 5 years from now. Let a represent the son's age today. Write an expression to represent the man's age today. Then find his age if his son is now 8 years old.

   _____

8. Let n represent an even integer. Write an expression for the sum of that number and the next three even integers after it. Simplify your expression fully.

   _____

9. A Fahrenheit temperature, F, can be converted to its corresponding Celsius temperature by subtracting 32° from that temperature and then multiplying the result by $\frac{5}{9}$. Write an expression that can be used to convert Fahrenheit temperatures to Celsius temperatures. Then find the Celsius temperature corresponding to 95 °F.

   _____

LESSON 2-2

Creating and Solving Equations

Practice and Problem Solving: A/B

Write an equation for each description.

1. 4 times a number is 16.

_____

2. A number minus 11 is 12.

_____

3. $\frac{9}{10}$ times a number plus 6 is 51.

_____

4. 3 times the sum of $\frac{1}{3}$ of a number and 8 is 11.

_____

Write and solve an equation to answer each problem.

5. Jan's age is 3 years less than twice Tritt's age. The sum of their ages is 30. Find their ages.

_____

6. Iris charges a fee for her consulting services plus an hourly rate that is $1\frac{1}{5}$ times her fee. On a 7-hour job, Iris charged $470. What is her fee and her hourly rate?

_____

7. When angles are complementary, the sum of their measures is 90 degrees. Two complementary angles have measures of $2x - 10$ degrees and $3x - 10$ degrees. Find the measures of each angle.

_____

8. Bill wants to rent a car. Rental Company A charges $35 per day plus $0.10 per mile driven. Rental Company B charges $25 per day plus $0.15 per mile driven. After how many miles driven will the price charged by each company be the same?

_____

9. Katie, Elizabeth, and Siobhan volunteer at the hospital. In a week, Katie volunteers 3 hours more than Elizabeth does and Siobhan volunteers 1 hour less than Elizabeth. Over 3 weeks, the number of hours Katie volunteers is equal to the sum of Elizabeth's and Siobhan's volunteer hours in 3 weeks. Complete the table to find out how many hours each person volunteers each week.

Volunteer	Volunteer Hours per week	Volunteer Hours over 3 weeks
Katie		
Elizabeth		
Siobhan		

LESSON 2-2 Creating and Solving Equations

Practice and Problem Solving: C

Write an equation for each description.

1. Eight times the difference of a number and 2 is the same as 3 times the sum of the number and 3.

   _____

2. The sum of –7 times a number and 8 times the sum of the number and 1 is the same as the number minus 7.

   _____

3. The quotient of the difference of a number and 24 divided by 8 is the same as the number divided by 6.

   _____

Write an equation for each situation. Then use the equation to solve the problem.

4. Sierra has a total of 61 dimes and quarters in her piggybank. She has 3 more quarters than dimes. The coins have a total value of $10.90. How many dimes and how many quarters does she have? [Hint: Use the decimal values of the c coins to write an equation.]

   _____

5. Penn used the formula for the sum of the angles inside a polygon: Sum of the interior angles = $(n - 2)180$, where n is the number of angles of the polygon. Penn's answer is 1,980 degrees. How many angles does the polygon have?

   _____

6. Fahrenheit temperature, F, can be found from a Celsius temperature, C, using the formula $F = 1.8C + 32$. Write an equation to find the temperature at which the Fahrenheit and Celsius readings are equal. Then find that temperature.

   _____

7. Amanda, Bryan, and Colin are in a book club. Amanda reads twice as many books as Bryan per month and Colin reads 4 fewer than 3 times as many books as Bryan in a month. In 4 months, the number of books Amanda reads is equal to $\dfrac{5}{8}$ the sum of the number of books Bryan and Colin read in 4 months. How many books does each person read each month?_____

Name	Books read in 1 month	Books read in 4 months
Amanda		
Bryan		
Colin		

LESSON 2-3 Solving for a Variable

Practice and Problem Solving: A/B

Solve the equation for the indicated variable.

1. $x = 3y$ for y

2. $m + 5n = p$ for m

3. $12r - 6s = t$ for r

_____   _____   _____

4. $21 = cd + e$ for d

5. $\dfrac{h}{j} = 15$ for j

6. $\dfrac{f - 7}{g} = h$ for f

_____   _____   _____

Solve the formula for the indicated variable.

7. Formula for the perimeter of a rectangle:
   $P = 2a + 2b$, for b

8. Formula for the circumference of a circle:
   $C = 2\pi r$, for r

_____   _____

9. Formula for the sum of angles of a triangle:
   $A + B + C = 180°$, for C

10. Formula for the volume of a cylinder:
    $V = \pi r^2 h$, for h

_____   _____

Solve.

11. Jill earns $15 per hour babysitting plus a transportation fee of $5 per job. Write a formula for E, Jill's earnings per babysitting job, in terms of h, the number of hours for a job. Then solve your formula for h.

_____

12. A taxi driver charges a fixed rate of r to pick up a passenger. In addition, the taxi driver charges a rate of m for each mile driven. Write a formula to represent T, the total amount this taxi driver will charge for a trip of n miles.

_____

13. Solve your formula from Problem 12 for m. Then find the taxi driver's hourly rate if his pickup rate is $2 and he charges $19.50 for a 7-mile trip.

_____

14. Describe when the formula for simple interest $I = prt$ would be more useful if it were rearranged.

_____

LESSON 2-3

Solving for a Variable

Practice and Problem Solving: C

Solve the equation for the indicated variable.

1. $y = \dfrac{3}{8}(x + 4)$ for x

2. $ab - ac = 2$ for a

3. $h - j = 4(h + j) - 7$ for h

_____ _____ _____

4. $n = m^2 - (n + 3)$

5. $\dfrac{d - e}{3d + e} = e$, for d

6. $\dfrac{q}{r} - 6 = q$, for r

_____ _____ _____

Solve the formula for the indicated variable.

7. Formula for centripetal force:

   $F = \dfrac{mv^2}{r}$, for m

8. Formula for the volume of a sphere:

   $V = \dfrac{4}{3}\pi r^3$, for r

_____ _____

9. Formula for half the volume of a right

   circular cylinder: $V = \dfrac{\pi r^2 h}{2}$, for r

10. Formula for focal length:

    $\dfrac{1}{V} = \dfrac{1}{U} + \dfrac{1}{F}$, for U

_____ _____

11. Pythagorean Theorem $a^2 + b^2 = c^2$:

    for a

12. Formula for the surface area of

    a cone: $S = \pi rs + \pi r^2$, for s

_____ _____

Solve.

13. Kinetic energy, K, equals the product of $\dfrac{1}{2}$, the mass of an object, m,

    and the square of its velocity, v. Write a formula for kinetic energy.
    Then solve your formula for v.

_____

14. In a circle, area and circumference can be found using the formulas

    $A = \pi r^2$ and $C = 2\pi r$, respectively. Write a formula for C in terms of
    A. (Your answer should not contain π.)

_____

15. Gina paid $131 for a car stereo on sale for 30% off. There was also
    7% sales tax on the purchase. Find the original price of the stereo.

_____

Creating and Solving Inequalities

LESSON 2-4

Practice and Problem Solving: A/B

Write an inequality for the situation.

1. Cara has $25 to buy dry pet food and treats for the animal shelter.
   A pound of dog food costs $2 and treats are $1 apiece. If she buys
   9 pounds of food, what is the greatest number of treats she can buy?

   _____

Solve each inequality for the value of the variable.

2. $2x \geq 6$

3. $\dfrac{a}{5} < 1$

   _____   _____

4. $5x + 7 \geq 2$

5. $5(z + 6) \leq 40$

   _____   _____

6. $5x \geq 7x + 4$

7. $3(b - 5) < -2b$

   _____   _____

Write and solve an inequality for each problem.

8. By selling old CDs, Sarah has a store credit for $153. A new CD costs
   $18. What are the possible numbers of new CDs Sarah can buy?

   _____

   _____

9. Ted needs an average of at least 70 on his three history tests. He has
   already scored 85 and 60 on two tests. What is the minimum grade
   Ted needs on his third test?

   _____

   _____

10. Jay can buy a stereo either online or at a local store. If he buys online,
    he gets a 15% discount, but has to pay a $12 shipping fee. At the local
    store, the stereo is not on sale, but there is no shipping fee. For what
    regular price is it cheaper for Jay to buy the stereo online?

    _____

    _____

LESSON 2-4

Creating and Solving Inequalities

Practice and Problem Solving: C

Write an inequality for the situation.

1. Miguel is buying 10 blankets for the animal shelter. If shipping each blanket costs $1.50 and Miguel has $75 to spend, what is the greatest amount he can spend for each blanket?

_____

Solve each inequality.

2. $2(x-3)+9 \geq x$

_____

3. $\frac{1}{2}a - 7 < \frac{2}{3}a - 9$

_____

4. $-10(9-2x)-x \leq 2x-5$

_____

5. $8\left(1-\frac{k}{2}\right) > -5k+17$

_____

6. $100-5(7-5y) > 5(7+5y)-100$

_____

7. $-6(w+3)-\frac{3w}{2} \leq -11-9w$

_____

Solve.

8. One car rental company charges $30 per day plus $0.25 per mile driven. A second company charges $40 per day plus $0.10 per mile driven. How many miles must you drive for a one-day rental at the second company to be less expensive than the same rental at the first company? Write an inequality to solve.

_____

9. To solve the inequality $\frac{2x-1}{x+8} > 1$, Hal multiplied both sides by $x+8$ and then got the solution $x > 9$. Is Hal's work correct?

_____

10. To solve $3 \geq 5-2x$, a student typically uses division by -2 and reverses the direction of the inequality. Show how to solve the inequality without using that step. Hint: Use the Addition Property of Equality.

_____

Name _____ Date _____ Class_____

Creating and Solving Compound Inequalities
Practice and Problem Solving: A/B

Solve each compound inequality and graph the solution.

1. $x > 2$ AND $x - 1 \leq 10$

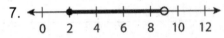

_____

2. $3x + 1 \geq -8$ AND $2x - 3 < 5$

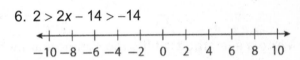

_____

3. $x > 10$ OR $x < 0$

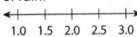

_____

4. $x - 1 > 11$ OR $3x \leq 21$

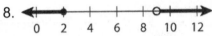

_____

5. $70 < 3x + 10 < 100$

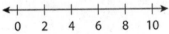

_____

6. $2 > 2x - 14 > -14$

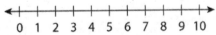

_____

Write the compound inequality shown by each graph.

7.

0 2 4 6 8 10 12

_____

8.

0 2 4 6 8 10 12

_____

Write a compound inequality to model the following situations. Graph the solution.

9. The forecast in Juneau, AK, calls for between 1.2 and 2.0 inches of rain.

1.0 1.5 2.0 2.5 3.0   _____

10. Water from industrial plants must be treated before entering the sewer system. Water that is too acidic or too basic will harm the pipes. A semiconductor manufacturer must adjust the pH of any waste water from the process to between 4.0 and 10.0.

0 2 4 6 8 10   _____

11. A welding shop figures a new welding machine will be cost effective if it runs less than 2 hours or more than 5.5 hours per day.

0 1 2 3 4 5 6 7 8 9 10   _____

Creating and Solving Compound Inequalities

LESSON 2-5

Practice and Problem Solving: C

Write the compound inequality, or inequalities. Draw and label a number line and graph the inequalities.

1. Pilots in the U.S. Air Force must meet certain height requirements. They must be at least 5 feet 4 inches tall, but not taller than 6 feet 2 inches. Convert the heights to inches before completing the problem.

   _____

2. Julie does her homework either between 4:00 and 6:00 p.m. or between 8:00 and 10:00 p.m.

   _____

Write a scenario that fits the compound inequality shown.

3.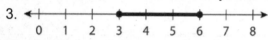

   _____

   _____

   _____

4.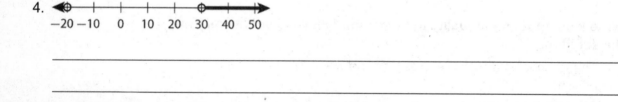

   _____

   _____

LESSON 3-1

Graphing Relationships

Practice and Problem Solving: A/B

Solve.

1. The graph shows the amount of rainfall during one storm. What does segment *d* represent?

   _____

   _____

2. Which segment represents the heaviest rainfall?

   _____

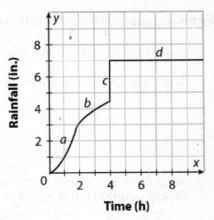

For each situation, tell whether a graph of the situation would be a continuous graph or a discrete graph.

3. the number of cans collected for recycling _____

4. pouring a glass of milk _____

5. the distance a car travels from a garage _____

6. the number of people in a restaurant _____

Identify which graph represents the situation, the kind of graph, and the domain and range of the graph.

7. Jason takes a shower, but the drain in the shower is not working properly.

a.
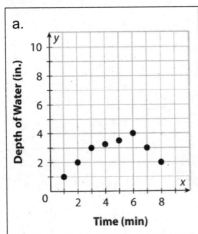

b.
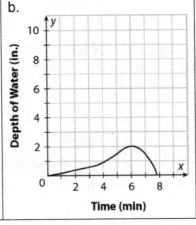

c.
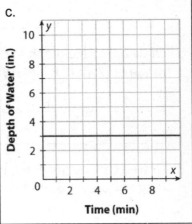

_____

LESSON
3-1

Graphing Relationships

Practice and Problem Solving: C

Sketch a graph for each situation. Be sure to label your graph.

1. Sherry read $\frac{1}{3}$ of a book, then went to bed.

   The next day she finished reading the entire book.

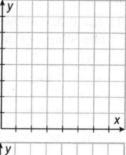

2. Simon counted the number of red trucks in each section of the parking lot at the mall.

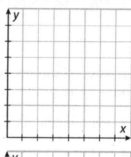

3. On Monday, the furniture truck made three deliveries within 8 miles of the warehouse.

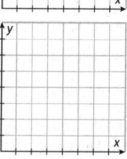

4. Write a situation for which you would use a discrete graph.

   _____

   _____

5. Draw a discrete graph that has a domain of $0 \le x \le 8$ and a range of {2, 4, 6, 8, 10}. Write a situation for the graph.

   _____

   _____

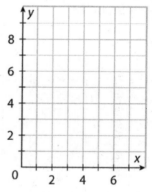

6. Draw a continuous graph that has a domain of $0 \le x \le 5$ and a range of $0 \le x \le 8$. Write a situation for the graph.

   _____

   _____

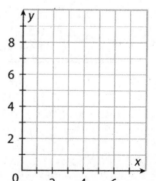

**LESSON
3-2**
Understanding Relations and Functions
Practice and Problem Solving: A/B

Express each relation as a table, as a graph, and as a mapping diagram.

1. {(−2, 5), (−1, 1), (3, 1), (−1, −2)}

x	y

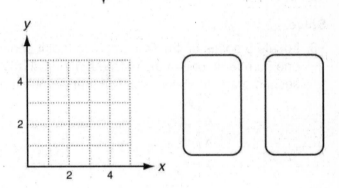

2. {(5, 3), (4, 3), (3, 3), (2, 3), (1, 3)}

x	y

Give the domain and range of each relation. Tell whether the relation is a function. Explain.

3.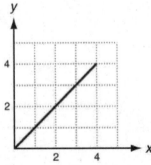

D: _____

R: _____

Function? _____

Explain: _____

_____

_____

_____

4.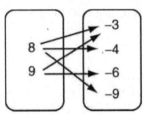

D: _____

R: _____

Function? _____

Explain: _____

_____

_____

_____

5.

x	y
1	4
2	5
0	6
1	7
2	8

D: _____

R: _____

Function? _____

Explain: _____

_____

_____

_____

LESSON
3-2
Understanding Relations and Functions
Practice and Problem Solving: C

Graph each relation. Then explain whether it is a function or not.

1. {(1, 2), (2, 2), (3, 3), (4, 3)}

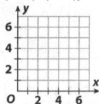

2. {(1, 5), (2, 4), (3, 5), (3, 4), (4, 4), (5, 5)}

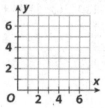

_____

_____

Solve.

3. Locate 5 points on the first graph so that it shows a function. Then change one number in one of the ordered pairs. Locate the new set of points on the second graph to show a relation that is not a function. Explain your strategy.

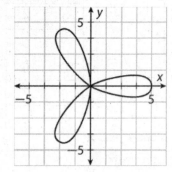   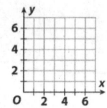

_____

4. Identify whether the graph shows a function or a relation that is not a function. Explain your reasoning.

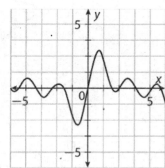   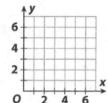

_____

5. The function INT(x) is used in spreadsheet programs. INT(x) takes any x and rounds it down to the nearest integer. Find INT(x) for x = 4.6, –2.3, and $\sqrt{2}$. Then find the domain and range.

_____

LESSON 3-3

Modeling with Functions
Practice and Problem Solving: A/B

Identify the dependent and independent variables in each situation.

1. The cost of a dozen eggs depends on the size of the eggs.

   dependent: _____   independent: _____

2. Ally works in a shop for $18 per hour.

   dependent: _____   independent: _____

3. 5 pounds of apples costs $7.45.

   dependent: _____   independent: _____

For each situation, write a function as a standard equation and in function notation.

4. Keesha will mow grass for $8 per hour.

   standard: _____   function: _____

5. Oranges are on sale for $1.59 per pound.

   standard: _____   function: _____

For each situation, identify the dependent and independent variables. Write a function in function notation, and use the function to solve the problem.

6. A plumber charges $70 per hour plus $40 for the call. What does he charge for 4 hours of work?

   dependent: _____   Solution: _____

   independent: _____   _____

   function: _____   _____

7. A sanitation company charges $4 per bag for garbage pickup plus a $10 weekly fee. A restaurant has 14 bags of *g* garbage. What will the sanitation company charge the restaurant?

   dependent: _____   Solution: _____

   independent: _____   _____

   function: _____   _____

Name _____ Date _____ Class_____

Modeling with Functions
Practice and Problem Solving: C

A range for each function is given. Find the domain values from the list: 1, 2, 3, 4, 5, 6, 7, 8. Explain how you arrived at your answer.

1. Function: $f(x) = -4x - 8$ R: {−16, −28, −36, −40}

   D: _____

   Explain: _____

   _____

2. Function: $f(x) = \dfrac{3}{2}x - 17$ R: {−15.5, −12.5, −9.5, −8}

   D: _____

   Explain: _____

   _____

3. Function: $f(x) = -\dfrac{1}{4}x + 2$ R: {1.5, 1, 0.25, 0}

   D: _____

   Explain: _____

   _____

4. Function: $f(x) = -5x - 13$ R: {−28, −38, −43, −48}

   D: _____

   Explain: _____

   _____

Solve.

5. A bakery has prepared 320 ounces of bread dough. A machine will cut the dough into 5-ounce sections and bake each section into a loaf. The amount of d dough left after m minutes is given by the function $d(m) = -5m + 320$. How many minutes will it take the machine to use all the dough? Find a reasonable domain and range for this situation.

   _____

   _____

   _____

Name _____ Date _____ Class_____

Graphing Functions
Practice and Problem Solving: A/B

Complete the table and graph the function for the given domain.

1. $f(x) = 3x - 2$ for $D = \{-3, 1, 5\}$

x	y
–3	
1	
5	

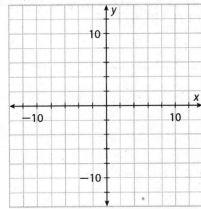

2. $y + 2x = 12$ for $D = \{2, 3, 4\}$

x	y
2	
3	
4	

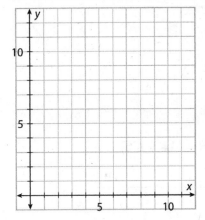

3. $3x - 3y = 9$ for $D = \{0 \leq x \leq 8\}$

x	y
0	
3	
8	

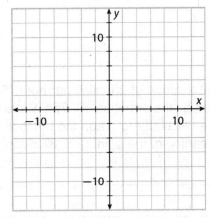

4. The function $h(d) = 2d + 4.3$ relates the h height of the water in a fountain in feet to the d diameter of the pipe carrying the water. Graph the function on a calculator and use the graph to find the height of the water when the pipe has a diameter of 1.5 inches.

_____

Name _____ Date _____ Class_____

Graphing Functions
Practice and Problem Solving: C

Determine the domain for each function. Then graph the function.

1. $f(x) = \frac{1}{2}x + 4$ for R = {5, 6, 7, 8}

   D = _____

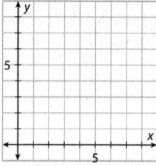

2. $6x - 3y = 12$ for R = {$-4 \leq y \leq 8$}

   D = _____

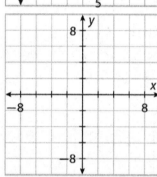

3. $3x = y - 4$ for R = {$4 \leq y \leq 8$}

   D = _____

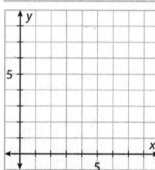

Solve.

4. A car travels at a speed of 25 miles per hour. The *d* distance it travels in *h* hours is given by the equation $d = 25h$. Write the equation as a function. Use a calculator to graph the function for the domain {$0 \leq h \leq 5$}. What is the meaning of the point (3.5, 87.5) on the graph?

   Function: _____

   Explain: _____

5. The formula for finding the distance traveled by a free-falling object is $D = 16t^2$, where *t* is the time in seconds. Use a calculator to graph this function for the domain {1, 2, 3, 4, 5, 6}. Find the range. Use the graph to find how much time it takes the object to fall 300 feet.

   Range: _____

   Explain: _____

Name _____ Date _____ Class_____

Identifying and Graphing Sequences
Practice and Problem Solving: A/B

Complete the table and state the domain and range for the sequence.

1.

n	1	2	☐	4	☐	6
$f(n)$	12	☐	36	☐	60	☐

Domain: _____

Range: _____

Write the first four terms of each sequence.

2. $f(n) = 3n - 1$

_____

3. $f(n) = n^2 + 2n + 5$

_____

4. $f(n) = (n-1)(n-2)$

_____

5. $f(n) = \sqrt{n-1}$

_____

Emma pays $10 to join a gym. For the first 5 months she pays a monthly $15 membership fee. For problems 6–7, use the explicit rule $f(n) = 15n + 10$.

6. Complete the table.

n	$f(n) = 15n + 10$	$f(n)$
1	$f(1) = 15\,(1) + 10 = 25$	25
2	$f(☐) = 15\,(☐) + ☐ = ☐$	☐
3	$f(☐) = 15\,(☐) + ☐ = ☐$	☐
4	$f(☐) = 15\,(☐) + ☐ = ☐$	☐
5	$f(☐) = 15\,(☐) + ☐ = ☐$	☐

Use the table to create ordered pairs.
The ordered pairs are

_____

_____

7. Graph the sequence using the ordered pairs.

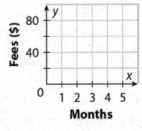

LESSON 4-1

Identifying and Graphing Sequences

Practice and Problem Solving: C

Find the first four terms of each sequence.

1. $f(n) = n^3 - n^2 + 1$

2. $f(n) = \dfrac{1}{n} - \dfrac{1}{n+1}$

_____

_____

3. $f(n) = \dfrac{n(n+1)(2n+1)}{6}$

4. $f(n) = \dfrac{n^2 - 1}{n^2 + 1}$

_____

_____

5. $f(n) = \dfrac{n}{12} - \dfrac{2}{3}$

6. $f(1) = 9,\ f(n) = 13 + \sqrt{f(n-1)}$ for $n \geq 2$

_____

_____

Graph the sequence that represents the situation on a coordinate plane.

7. Rebecca had $100 in her savings account in the first week. She adds $45 each week for 5 weeks. The savings account balance can be shown by a sequence.

8. Adam has $300 to donate. For the next five weeks he donates $60 each week to a different charity. His remaining donation money can be shown by a sequence.

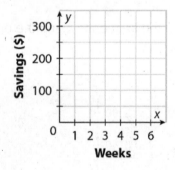

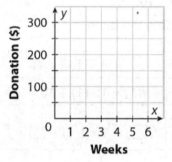

Solve.

9. In the Fibonacci sequence, $f(1) = 1$, $f(2) = 1$, and $f(n) = f(n-2) + f(n-1)$ for $n \geq 3$. Find the first 10 terms of the Fibonacci sequence.

_____

10. Use $f(n)$ from Problem 9 to create a new sequence: $r(n) = \dfrac{f(n)}{f(n+1)}$.

Write the first eight terms of this sequence as decimals. If necessary, round a term to three decimal places. Explain any patterns you see.

_____

LESSON 4-2

Constructing Arithmetic Sequences

Practice and Problem Solving: A/B

Write an explicit rule and a recursive rule using the table.

1.

n	1	2	3	4	5
f(n)	8	12	16	20	24

_____

_____

2.

n	1	2	3	4	5
f(n)	11	7	3	−1	−5

_____

_____

3.

n	1	2	3	4	5
f(n)	−20	−13	−6	1	8

_____

_____

4.

n	1	2	3	4	5
f(n)	2.7	4.3	5.9	7.5	9.1

_____

_____

Write an explicit rule and a recursive rule using the sequence.

5. 45, 50, 55, 60, 65

_____

_____

6. 94, 87, 80, 73, 66

_____

_____

7. 12, 26, 40, 54, 68

_____

_____

8. 83, 43, 3, −37, −77

_____

_____

Solve.

9. The explicit rule for an arithmetic sequence is $f(n) = 13 + 6(n − 1)$.
   Find the first four terms of the sequence.

_____

10. Helene paid back $100 in Month 1 of her loan. In each month after that,
    Helene paid back $50. The graph shows the sequence. Write an explicit rule.

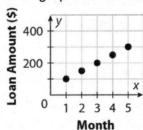

_____

LESSON 4-2

Constructing Arithmetic Sequences

Practice and Problem Solving: C

Write an explicit rule and a recursive rule for each sequence.

1.

n	1	2	3	4	5
$f(n)$	−3.4	−2.1	−0.8	0.5	1.8

_____

_____

2.

n	1	2	3	4	5
$f(n)$	$\frac{1}{6}$	$\frac{1}{4}$	$\frac{1}{3}$	$\frac{5}{12}$	$\frac{1}{2}$

_____

_____

3.

n	1	3	5	6	9
$f(n)$	82	81	80	79.5	78

_____

_____

4.

n	1	4	8	13	19
$f(n)$	−22	2	34	74	122

_____

_____

Solve.

5. A recursive rule for an arithmetic sequence is $f(1) = -8$, $f(n) = f(n-1) - 6.5$ for $n \geq 2$. Write an explicit rule for this sequence.

_____

6. The third and thirtieth terms of an arithmetic sequence are 4 and 85. Write an explicit rule for this sequence.

_____

7. $f(n) = 900 - 60(n-1)$ represents the amount Oscar still needs to repay on a loan at the beginning of month n. Find the amount Oscar pays monthly and the month in which he will make his last payment.

_____

8. Find the first six terms of the sequence whose explicit formula is $f(n) = (-1)^n$. Explain whether it is an arithmetic sequence.

_____

9. An arithmetic sequence has common difference of 5.6 and its tenth term is 75. Write a recursive formula for this sequence.

_____

10. The cost of a college's annual tuition follows an arithmetic sequence. The cost was $35,000 in 2010 and $40,000 in 2012. According to this sequence, what will tuition be in 2020?

_____

Name _____ Date _____ Class _____

LESSON 4-3

Modeling with Arithmetic Sequences

Practice and Problem Solving: A/B

Complete the table of values to determine the common difference.

1. Mia drives 55 miles per hour. The total miles driven is given by the function $C(m) = 55m$.

Hours	1	2	3	4
Distance in miles				

Common difference: _____

2. Each pound of potatoes costs $1.20. The total cost, in dollars, is given by the function $C(p) = 1.2p$.

Pounds	1	2	3	4
Cost in dollars				

Common difference: _____

Solve. Use the following for 3–7.

Riley buys a swim pass for the pool in January. The first month costs $30. Each month after that, the cost is $20 per month. Riley wants to swim through December.

3. Complete the table of values.

Months	1	2	3	4	5	6	7	8	9	10	11	12
Cost in dollars	30	50	70									

4. What is the common difference?

_____

5. Write the equation for finding the total cost of a one-year swim pass.

_____

6. What does $f(12)$ represent?

_____

7. What is the total amount of money Riley will spend for a one-year swim pass?

_____

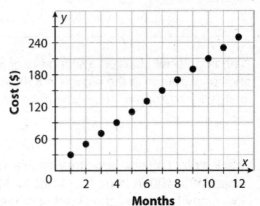

LESSON
4-3

Modeling with Arithmetic Sequences

Practice and Problem Solving: C

Use the following diagram for 1–3.

1   2   3   4   5   6   7   8

1. How many sides will Figure 8 have? Is it shaded?

    _____

2. Make a table to show the sequence of figures.

Figure						
Number of Sides						

3. How many sides will Figure 21 have? Is it shaded?

    _____

4. Is the sequence of figures an arithmetic sequence? Explain.

    _____

Solve.

5. A movie rental club charges $4.95 for the first month's rentals. The club charges $18.95 for each additional month. What is the total cost for one year?

    _____

6. A photographer charges a sitting fee of $69.95 for one person. Each additional person in the picture is $30. What is the total sitting fee charge for a group of 10 people to be photographed?

    _____

7. Grant is planting one large tree and several smaller trees. He has a budget of $1400. A large tree costs $200. Each smaller tree is $150. How many total trees can Grant purchase on his budget?

    _____

Name _____ Date _____ Class_____

Understanding Linear Functions

Practice and Problem Solving: A/B

Tell whether each function is linear or not.

1. $y = 3x^2$

2. $7 - y = 5x + 11$

3. $-2(x + y) + 9 = 1$

_____   _____   _____

Complete the tables. Is the change constant for equal intervals? If so, what is the change?

4. $3x + 5y = 4$

x	−1	0	1	2
y	$\frac{7}{5}$			

Constant? _____

Change? _____

5. $4x^2 + y = 4$

x	−1	0	1	2
y	0	4		

Constant? _____

Change? _____

6. $6x + 1 = y$

x	−1	0	1	2
y				

Constant? _____

Change? _____

Graph each line.

7. $y = \frac{1}{2}x - 3$

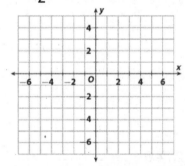

8. $2x + 3y = 8$

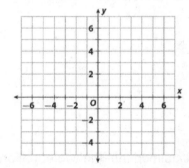

The solid and dashed lines show how two consultants charge for their services. Use the graph for 9–11.

9. How much does each charge for a 6-hour job?

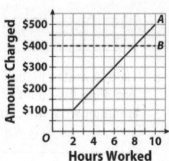

_____

10. Does either consultant charge according to a linear function?

_____

11. For which length of job do *A* and *B* charge the same amount?

_____

12. Are the functions discrete or continuous? Explain. _____

LESSON
5-1
Understanding Linear Functions
Practice and Problem Solving: C

Tell what constant amount the function changes by over equal intervals.

1. $3x + 4y = 24$

2. $y = -5x + 10$

_____

3. $x - 7y - 15 = 0$

4. $9x - \dfrac{2}{3}y = -4$

_____

Graph each line.

5. $6x + 5y = 30$

6. $3(x + y) - 2(x - y) = 5(8 + 3y)$

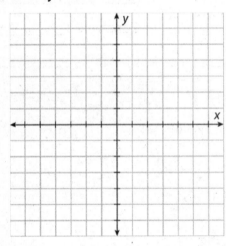

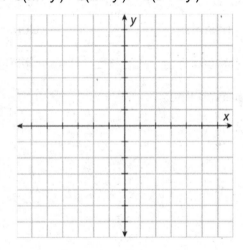

Solve.

7. A student claimed that the two equations $\dfrac{y-8}{x-1} = 2$ and $y = 2x + 6$
   have identical lines as their graphs. Do you agree? Explain.

_____

_____

8. A line is written in the form $Ax + By = 0$, where A and B are not both
   zero. Find the coordinates of the point that must lie on this line,
   no matter what the choice of A and B.

_____

9. A line is written in the form $Ax + By = C$, where $A \neq 0$. Find the
   x-coordinate of the point on the line at which $y = 3$.

_____

LESSON 5-2

Using Intercepts

Practice and Problem Solving: A/B

Find each *x*- and *y*-intercept.

1.
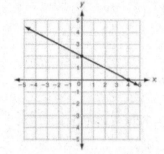

2.
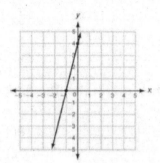

3.
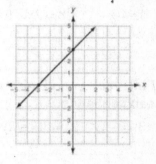

_____

_____

_____

_____

_____

_____

Use intercepts to graph the line described by each equation.

4. $3x + 2y = -6$

5. $x - 4y = 4$

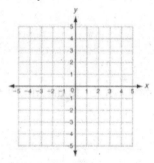

6. At a fair, hamburgers sell for $3.00 each and hot dogs sell for $1.50 each. The equation $3x + 1.5y = 30$ describes the number of hamburgers and hot dogs a family can buy with $30.

   a. Find the intercepts and graph the function.

    _____

   b. What does each intercept represent?

    _____

    _____

    _____

    _____

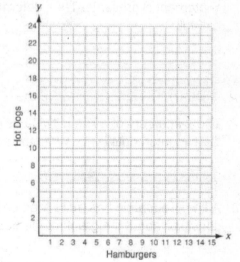

LESSON 5-2

Using Intercepts

Practice and Problem Solving: C

Find each *x*- and *y*-intercept.

1. $4(x - y) + 3 = 2x - 5$

2. $5x + 9y = 18 - (x + y)$

_____   _____

Find each *x*- and *y*-intercept. Then graph the line described by each equation.

3. $x - (y + 2) = 3(x - 2y + 1)$

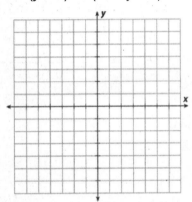

4. $8(4 + x) - 3 = 12(x + y) + 5$

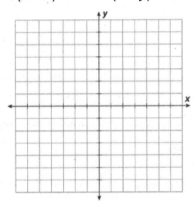

Solve.

5. Write the equations of three distinct lines that have the same *y*-intercept, −1.

_____

6. A home uses 8 gallons of oil each day for heat. If its oil storage tank is filled to 275 gallons, the function $y = 275 - 8x$ represents the number of gallons remaining in the tank after *x* days of use. Explain what the *x*-intercept represents. Then determine when the tank will be half-full.

_____

_____

7. The *x*-intercept of a line is twice as great as its *y*-intercept. The sum of the two intercepts is 15. Write the equation of the line in standard form.

_____

8. A linear equation has more than one *y*-intercept. What can you conclude about the graph of the equation?

_____

Name _____ Date _____ Class _____

Interpreting Rate of Change and Slope

Practice and Problem Solving: A/B

**Find the rise and run between the marked points on each graph.
Then find the rate of change or slope of the line.**

1.

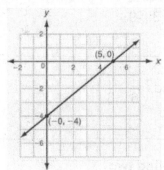

2.

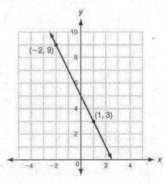

3.

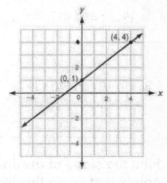

rise = _____ run = _____   rise = _____ run = _____   rise = _____ run = _____

slope = _____   slope = _____   slope = _____

Find the slope of each line. Tell what the slope represents.

4.

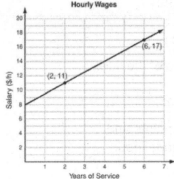

5.

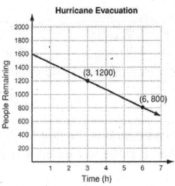

_____   _____

_____   _____

Solve.

6. When ordering tickets online, a college theater charges a $5 handling
   fee no matter how large the order. Tickets to a comedy concert cost
   $58 each. If you had to graph the line showing the total cost, *y*, of
   buying *x* tickets, what would the slope of your line be? Explain
   your thinking.

_____

_____

LESSON
5-3

Interpreting Rate of Change and Slope

Practice and Problem Solving: C

Find the rate of change or slope of the line containing each pair of points.

1. (4, 5) and (11, 33)

_____

2. (–4, 8) and (3, –9)

_____

3. (0, –8) and (3, 3)

_____

4. $\left(\dfrac{1}{4}, \dfrac{1}{2}\right)$ and $\left(\dfrac{1}{6}, \dfrac{1}{3}\right)$

_____

Find the slope of the line represented by each equation. First find two points that lie on the line. Then find the rate of change or slope.

5. $2x + y = 5$

_____

6. $3x - 5y = 17$

_____

7. $y = 4 - 9x$

_____

8. $y + 5 = 1$

_____

9. $-x + 4y = 12$

_____

10. $6(x - y) = 5(x + y)$

_____

Solve.

11. A line has *x*-intercept of 6 and *y*-intercept of –4. Find the slope of the line.

_____

12. A vertical line contains the points (3, 2) and (3, 6). Use these points and the formula for slope to explain why a vertical line's slope is undefined.

_____

_____

13. The steepness of a road is called its grade. The higher the grade, the steeper the road. For example, an interstate highway is considered out of standard if its grade exceeds 7%. Interpret a grade of 7% in terms of slope. Use feet to explain the meaning for a driver.

_____

_____

14. Ariel was told the *x*-intercept and the *y*-intercept of a line with a positive slope. Yet, it was impossible for Ariel to find the slope of the line. What can you conclude about this line? Explain your thinking.

_____

_____

LESSON
6-1

Slope-Intercept Form

Practice and Problem Solving: A/B

Write the equation for each line in slope-intercept form. Then identify the slope and the *y*-intercept.

1. $4x + y = 7$

    Equation: _____

    Slope: _____

    y-intercept: _____

2. $2x - 3y = 9$

    Equation: _____

    Slope: _____

    y-intercept: _____

3. $5x + 1 = 4y + 7$

    Equation: _____

    Slope: _____

    y-intercept: _____

4. $3x + 2y = 2x + 8$

    Equation: _____

    Slope: _____

    y-intercept: _____

Graph the line described by each equation.

5. $y = -3x + 4$

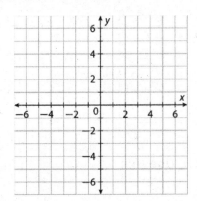

6. $y = \dfrac{5}{6}x - 1$

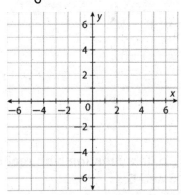

Solve.

7. What are the slope and *y*-intercept of $y = 3x - 5$?

    _____

8. A line has a *y*-intercept of −11 and slope of 0.25. Write its equation in slope-intercept form.

    _____

9. A tank can hold 30,000 gallons of water. If 500 gallons of water are used each day, write the equation that represents the amount of water in the tank *x* days after it is full.

    _____

Slope-Intercept Form

LESSON 6-1

Practice and Problem Solving: C

Write the equation for each line in slope-intercept form. Then identify the slope and the *y*-intercept.

1. $3(x - 2y) = 5(x - 3y) + 9$

   Equation: _____

   Slope: _____

   y-intercept: _____

2. $\dfrac{x}{5} - \dfrac{y}{7} = 1$

   Equation: _____

   Slope: _____

   y-intercept: _____

Write an equation for each line. Then graph the line.

3. A line whose slope and *y*-intercept are equal and the sum of the two is −4

   _____

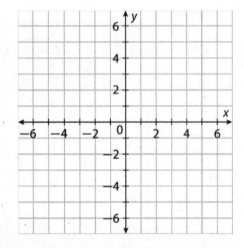

4. A line that has a slope half as great as its *y*-intercept and the sum of the two is 1

   _____

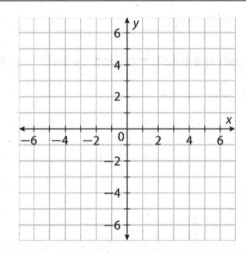

Let $f(x) = mx + b$ be a function with real numbers for *m* and *b*. Use this for Problems 5 and 6.

5. Show that the domain of this function is the set of all real numbers.

   _____

   _____

6. Show that the range of the function may or may not be the set of all real numbers.

   _____

   _____

   _____

   _____

LESSON 6-2

Point-Slope Form

Practice and Problem Solving: A/B

Write each in point-slope form.

1. Line with a slope of 2 and passes through point (3, 5).

   _____

2. Line with a slope of –3 and passes through point (–1, 7).

   _____

3. (–6, 3) and (4, 3) are on the line.

   _____

4. (0, 0) and (5, 2) are on the line.

   _____

5.

x	y
0	0
2	9
4	18

_____

6.

x	y
–2	18
1	9
4	0

_____

7.

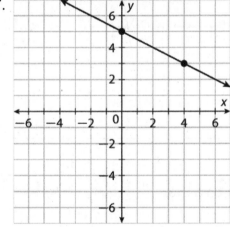

_____

8.

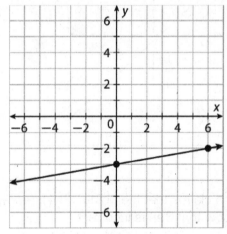

_____

Solve.

9. For 4 hours of work, a consultant charges $400. For 5 hours of work, she charges $450. Write a point-slope equation to show this, then find the amount she will charge for 10 hours of work.

   _____

   _____

LESSON
6-2
Point-Slope Form
Practice and Problem Solving: C

Write each in point-slope form.

1. The graph of the function has slope of $-\dfrac{3}{4}$ and contains $\left(-2, -\dfrac{8}{5}\right)$.

_____

2. The graph of the function has slope of $\dfrac{2}{5}$ and contains $(-35, 39)$.

_____

3.

x	y
$\dfrac{1}{6}$	−5
$\dfrac{1}{2}$	−10

_____

4.

x	y
1	$-\dfrac{2}{3}$
$\dfrac{2}{3}$	2

_____

5.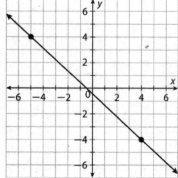

_____

6.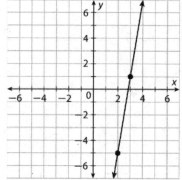

_____

Solve.

7. Ben claims that the points (2, 4), (4, 8), and (8, 12) lie on a line.
   Show that Ben is incorrect.

_____

_____

8. Prove the following statement: If the *x*- and *y*-intercepts of a line are identical nonzero numbers, the line must have a slope of −1.

_____

_____

9. A consignment store charges a flat rate plus a percent of the sale price for any items it sells. An item priced at $500 carries a total fee of $120 while an item priced at $800 carries a total fee of $180. Use the point-slope equation to find the total fee for an item priced at $300.

_____

Name _____ Date _____ Class_____

Standard Form
Practice and Problem Solving: A/B

Tell whether each function is written in standard form. If not, rewrite it in standard form.

1. $y = 3x$

2. $7 - y = 5x + 11$

3. $-2(x + y) + 9 = 1$

_____

_____

_____

_____

_____

_____

Given a slope and a point, write an equation in standard form for each line.

4. slope = 6, (3, 7)

5. slope = -1, (2, 5)

6. slope = 9, (-5, 2)

_____

_____

_____

Graph the line of each equation.

7. $x - 2y = 6$

8. $2x + 3y = 8$

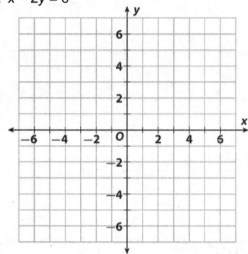

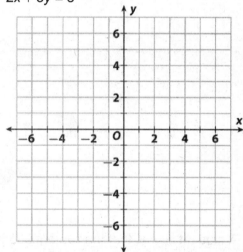

Solve.

9. A swimming pool was filling with water at a constant rate of 200 gallons per hour. The pool had 50 gallons before the timer started. Write an equation in standard form to model the situation.

_____

10. A grocery bag containing 4 potatoes weighs 2 pounds. An identical bag that contains 12 potatoes weighs 4 pounds. Write an equation in standard form that shows the relationship of the weight (y) and the number of potatoes (x).

_____

LESSON 6-3

Standard Form
Practice and Problem Solving: C

Write each equation in slope-intercept form. Then identify its intercepts.

1. $3x + 4y = 24$

2. $y = -5x + 10$

_____

_____

3. $x - 7y - 15 = 0$

4. $9x - \dfrac{2}{3}y = -4$

_____

_____

Graph each line. Rewrite the equation in standard form if necessary.

5. $6x + 5y = 30$

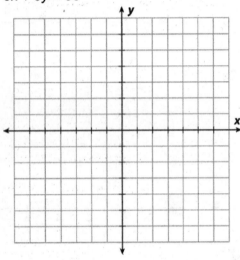

6. $3(x + y) - 2(x - y) = 5(8 + 3y)$

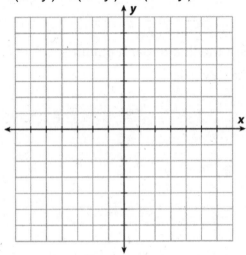

Solve.

7. A student claims that the two equations $\dfrac{y-8}{x-1} = 2$ and $y = 2x + 6$ have identical lines as their graphs. Do you agree? Explain.

_____

_____

8. A line is written in standard form $Ax + By = 0$, where A and B are not both zero. Find the coordinates of the point that must lie on this line, no matter what the choice of A and B.

_____

9. A line is written in standard form $Ax + By = C$, where $A \neq 0$. Find the x-coordinate of the point on the line at which $y = 3$.

_____

LESSON	**Transforming Linear Functions**
6-4	

Practice and Problem Solving: A/B

Identify the steeper line.

1. $y = 3x + 4$ or $y = 6x + 11$

2. $y = -5x - 1$ or $y = -2x - 7$

_____ _____

Each transformation is performed on the line with the equation $y = 2x - 1$. Write the equation of the new line.

3. vertical translation down 3 units

4. slope increased by 4

_____ _____

5. slope divided in half

6. shifted up 1 unit

_____ _____

7. slope increased by 50%

8. shifted up 3 units and slope doubled

_____ _____

A salesperson earns a base salary of $4000 per month plus 15% commission on sales. Her monthly income, $f(s)$, is given by the function $f(s) = 4000 + 0.15s$, where s is monthly sales, in dollars. Use this information for Problems 9–12.

9. Find $g(s)$ if the salesperson's commission is lowered to 5%.

_____

10. Find $h(s)$ if the salesperson's base salary is doubled.

_____

11. Find $k(s)$ if the salesperson's base salary is cut in half and her commission is doubled.

_____

12. Graph $f(s)$ and $k(s)$ on the coordinate grid below.

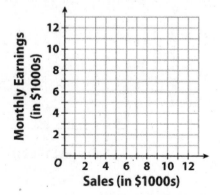

LESSON 6-4 **Transforming Linear Functions**

Practice and Problem Solving: C

Identify the steeper line.

1. $y = 2x - 3$ or $x - 5y = 20$

_____

2. $x + 10y = 1$ or $3x + 20y = 1$

_____

Each transformation is performed on the line with the equation $y = 4x - 20$. Write the equation of the new line.

3. slope cut in half

_____

4. vertical translation 25 units upward

_____

5. shifted up 8 units and slope tripled

_____

6. reflection across the y-axis

_____

Solve.

7. Compare the steepness of the lines whose equations are $8x + y = 1$ and $-8x + y = 2$. Explain your reasoning.

_____

_____

8. $f(x)$ is an increasing linear function that passes through the point (4, 0). Show that if written in the form $f(x) = mx + b$, $m > 0$ and $b < 0$.

_____

_____

9. A salesperson earns a base salary of $400 per week plus 20% commission on sales. He is offered double his base salary if he'll accept half his original commission. Graph and label the original deal and the new deal below. Next to the graph, find when the original deal is a better choice. Explain your thinking.

_____

_____

_____

_____

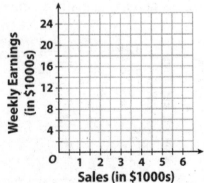

LESSON
6-5
Comparing Properties of Linear Functions
Practice and Problem Solving: A/B

The linear functions *f*(*x*) and *g*(*x*) are defined by the graph and table below. Assume that the domain of *g*(*x*) includes all real numbers between the least and greatest values of *x* shown in the table.

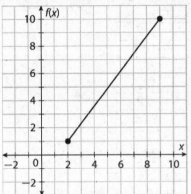

x	g(x)
1	35
2	30
3	25
4	20
5	15
6	10
7	5
8	0

1. Find the domain of *f*(*x*).

   _____

2. Find the domain of *g*(*x*).

   _____

3. Find the range of *f*(*x*).

   _____

4. Find the range of *g*(*x*).

   _____

5. Find the initial value of *f*(*x*).

   _____

6. Find the initial value of *g*(*x*).

   _____

7. Find the slope of the line represented by *f*(*x*).

   _____

8. Find the slope of the line represented by *g*(*x*).

   _____

9. How are *f*(*x*) and *g*(*x*) alike? How are they different?

   _____

10. Describe a situation that could be represented by *f*(*x*).

   _____

11. Describe a situation that could be represented by *g*(*x*).

   _____

12. If the domains of *f*(*x*) and *g*(*x*) were extended to include all real numbers greater than or equal to 0, what would their *y*-intercepts be?

   _____

Comparing Properties of Linear Functions

LESSON 6-5

Practice and Problem Solving: C

The linear functions $f(x)$, $g(x)$, $h(x)$, and $k(x)$ are defined by the graphs and table below. Assume that the domains of $h(x)$ and $k(x)$ include all real numbers between the least and greatest values of x shown in the table.

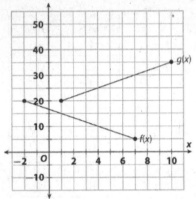

x	h(x)	k(x)
1	2.5	12
2	5	14.5
3	7.5	17
4	10	19.5
5	12.5	22
6	15	24.5
7	17.5	27
8	20	29.5
9	22.5	32
10	25	34.5

1. Find the domains of the functions.

   _____

2. Find the ranges of the functions.

   _____

3. Find the initial values of the functions.

   _____

4. Find the slopes of the functions.

   _____

5. Describe a situation that could be represented by two of the functions.

   _____

   _____

6. If the domains of the functions were extended to include all real numbers greater than or equal to 0, what would their y-intercepts be?

   _____

7. If the domain of $f(x)$ and $g(x)$ were extended to include all real numbers, at what point would their graphs intersect?

   _____

LESSON 7-1

Modeling Linear Relationships

Practice and Problem Solving: A/B

Solve.

1. A recycling center pays $0.10 per aluminum can and $0.05 per plastic bottle. The cheerleading squad wants to raise $500.

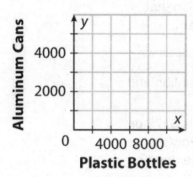

   a. Write a linear equation that describes the problem.

   _____

   b. Graph the linear equation.

   c. If the cheerleading squad collects 6000 plastic bottles, how many cans will it need to collect to reach the goal?

   _____

2. A bowling alley charges $2.00 per game and will rent a pair of shoes for $1.00 for any number of games. The bowling alley has an earnings goal of $300 for the day.

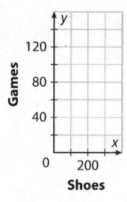

   a. Write a linear equation that describes the problem.

   _____

   b. Graph the linear equation.

   c. If the bowling alley rents 40 pairs of shoes, how many games will need to be played to reach its goal?

   _____

3. The members of a wheelchair basketball league are playing a benefit game to meet their fundraising goal of $900. Tickets cost $15 and snacks cost $6.

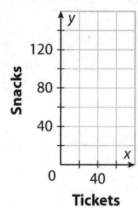

   a. Write a linear equation that describes the problem.

   _____

   b. Graph the linear equation.

   c. If the team sells 50 tickets, how many snacks does it need to sell to reach the goal?

   _____

LESSON 7-1

Modeling Linear Relationships

Practice and Problem Solving: C

Solve.

1. Mr. Malone can heat his house in the winter by burning three cords of wood, by using natural gas, or by a combination of the two. His heating budget for the winter is $600.

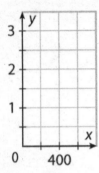

a. Write a linear equation that describes the problem.

_____

b. Graph the linear equation and label both axes.

c. If Mr. Malone spends $275 on natural gas, about how many cords of wood will he need?

_____

2. Timber Hill Tennis Club sells monthly memberships for $72 and tennis rackets for $150 each. The tennis club has a sales goal of $5400 per month.

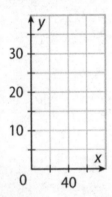

a. Write a linear equation that describes the problem.

_____

b. Graph the linear equation and label both axes.

c. If the club sells 50 memberships, how many rackets must be sold to meet the goal?

_____

3. Brian's Bakery sells loaves of Italian bread for $3.50 and loaves of rye bread for $2.80. Brian's goal is to bring in $420 per day from sales of these two items.

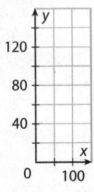

a. Write a linear equation that describes the problem.

_____

b. Graph the linear equation and label both axes.

c. If Brian sells 100 Italian loaves, how many rye loaves must he sell to meet his goal?

_____

LESSON 7-2 Using Functions to Solve One-Variable Equations

Practice and Problem Solving: A/B

Use the following for 1–5.

Locksmith Larry charges $90 for a house call plus $20 per hour.
Locksmith Barry charges $50 for a house call plus $30 per hour.

1. Write a one-variable equation for the charges of Locksmith Larry.

   $f(x) =$ _____

2. Write a one-variable equation for the charges of Locksmith Barry.

   $g(x) =$ _____

3. Complete the table for $f(x)$ and $g(x)$.

Hours	$f(x)$	$g(x)$
0		
1		
2		
3		
4		
5		

4. Plot $f(x)$ and $g(x)$ on the graph below. Find the intersection.

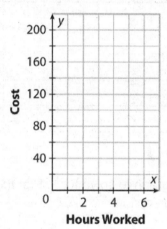

5. After how many hours will the two locksmiths charge the same

   amount? _____

6. Jill has $600 in savings. She has a recurring monthly bill of $75 but no income.

   a. Write an equation, $f(x)$, representing her savings each month.

      _____

   b. Let $g(x) = 0$ represent the point when Jill has no money left. In how many months, x, will her savings account reach zero?

      _____

Name _____ Date _____ Class_____

Using Functions to Solve One-Variable Equations
Practice and Problem Solving: C

Use the following for 1–5.

DJ A charges $75.30 plus $12.50 per hour. DJ B charges $52.90 plus
$18.10 per hour. When will their charges be equal?

1. Write a one-variable equation for the charges of DJ A.

   $f(x) =$ _____

2. Write a one-variable equation for the charges of DJ B.

   $g(x) =$ _____

3. Complete the table for $f(x)$ and $g(x)$.

Hours	$f(x)$	$g(x)$
0		
1		
2		
3		
4		
5		

4. Use a graph to solve for x. Plot $f(x)$ and $g(x)$ on the graph below. Find
   the intersection.

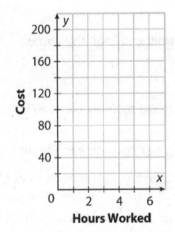

Hours Worked

5. After how many hours will the two DJs charge the same

   amount? _____

LESSON 7-3

Linear Inequalities in Two Variables

Practice and Problem Solving: A/B

Use substitution to tell whether each ordered pair is a solution of the given inequality.

1. $(3, 4); y > x + 2$

2. $(4, 2); y \le 2x - 3$

3. $(2, -1); y < -x$

_____   _____   _____

Rewrite each linear inequality in slope-intercept form. Then graph the solutions in the coordinate plane.

4. $y - x \le 3$

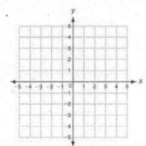

5. $6x + 2y > -2$

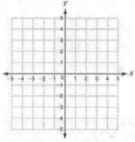

_____   _____

6. Trey is buying peach and blueberry yogurt cups. He will buy at most 8 cups of yogurt. Let x be the number of peach yogurt cups and y be the number of blueberry yogurt cups he buys.

   a. Write an inequality to describe the situation.

   _____

   b. Graph the solutions.

   c. Give two possible combinations of peach and blueberry yogurt that Trey can choose.

   _____

   _____

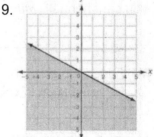

Write an inequality to represent each graph.

7.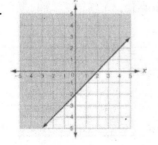

8.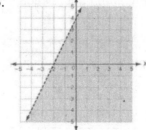

9.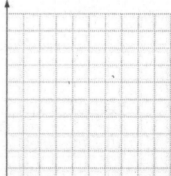

_____   _____   _____

**LESSON
7-3**

Linear Inequalities in Two Variables

Practice and Problem Solving: C

Graph the solution set for each inequality.

1. $2x - 3y \le 15$

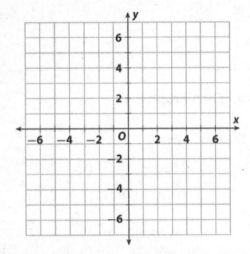

2. $\dfrac{1}{4}x + \dfrac{1}{3}y < \dfrac{1}{2}$

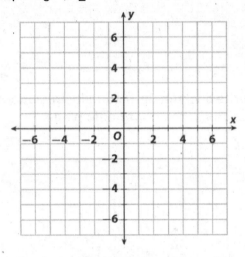

Write and graph an inequality for each situation.

3. Hats (x) cost $5 and scarves ($y$) cost $8. Joel can spend at most $40.

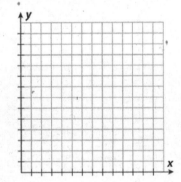

4. Juana wants to sell more than 1 million dollars worth of $1000 laptops ($x$) and $2000 desktop computers ($y$) this year.

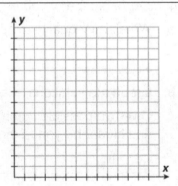

Solve.

5. To graph $y \le 2x + 8$, you first draw the line $y = 2x + 8$. Explain how you can then tell, *without doing any arithmetic*, which region to shade.

_____

6. Why does the graph of $y \ge x$ contain a solid line while the graph of $y > x$ contains a dotted line?

_____

Two-Way Frequency Tables

LESSON 8-1

Practice and Problem Solving: A/B

Solve.

1. Nancy's school conducted a recycling drive. Students collected 20-pound bags of plastic, glass, and metal containers. The first chart shows the data: the bags of each type of container that were collected. Complete the frequency table.

20-pound Bags Collected
glass glass plastic metal
plastic plastic metal glass
glass plastic metal metal
metal glass glass plastic
plastic plastic plastic metal

Bags containing	Frequency
plastic	
glass	

2. A school administrator conducted a survey in her school. Students were asked to choose the science or the natural history museum for an upcoming field trip. Complete the two-way frequency table.

	Field Trip Preferences		
Gender	Science	History	Total
Boys		56	102
Girls	54		
Total			200

3. Teresa surveyed 100 students about whether they wanted to join the math club or the science club. Thirty-eight students wanted to join the math club only, 34 wanted to join the science club only, 21 wanted to join both math and science clubs, and 7 did not want to join either. Complete the two-way frequency table.

	Science		
Math	Yes	No	Total
Yes		38	
No	34		
Total			

4. A pet-shop owner surveyed 200 customers about whether they own a cat or a dog. Partial results of the survey are recorded below. Complete the two-way frequency table.

   One-half of the respondents own a dog but not a cat.

   The number of customers who own neither a dog nor a cat is 38.

   There are no customers who own both a dog and a cat.

	Cat		
Dog	Yes	No	Total
Yes	0		
No		38	
Total			

LESSON 8-1
Two-Way Frequency Tables
Practice and Problem Solving: C

1. A surveyor asked students whether they favored or did not favor a change in the Friday lunch menu at their school.
   - The survey involved 200 students.
   - The number of boys surveyed equaled the number of girls surveyed.
   - Fifty percent of the girls favored the change.
   - The number of boys who did not favor the change was two-thirds of the number of boys who favored the change.

   Complete the two-way frequency table. Explain your reasoning.

Gender	Favor or Disfavor the Change		
	Yes	No	Total
Girls			
Boys			
Total			

   _____

   _____

   _____

2. A pet-shop owner surveyed 150 customers about whether they owned birds, cats, or dogs. Partial results of the survey are recorded below. In the table, B represents bird, C represents cat, and D represents dog.

Reply	Ownership								
	B	C	D	B and C Only	B and D Only	C and D Only	B, C, D	Not B, C, or D	Total
Yes	80	77	84	32	30	29	12	6	150
No	70	73	66	128	120	121	138	144	150
Total	150	150	150	150	150	150	150	150	150

   Write the correct number in each of the eight regions in the Venn diagram below.

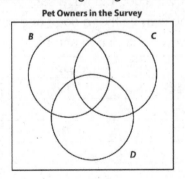

Pet Owners in the Survey

Name _____ Date _____ Class _____

 LESSON 8-2 # Relative Frequency and Probability
Practice and Problem Solving: A/B

The two-way frequency table below represents the results of a survey
about favorite forms of entertainment. In Exercises 1–3, write
fractions that are not simplified as responses.

	Like Board Games		
Like Reading	**Yes**	**No**	**Total**
Yes	48	25	73
No	43	9	52
Total	91	34	125

1. Find the joint relative frequency of people surveyed who like
   to read but dislike playing board games.   _____

2. What is the marginal relative frequency of people surveyed who
   like to read?   _____

3. Given someone interested in reading, is that person more or less likely
   to take an interest in playing board games? Explain.

   _____

   _____

4. Given someone interested in board games, is that person more or less
   likely to take an interest in reading? Explain your response.

   _____

   _____

The two-way frequency table below represents the results of a survey
about ways students get to school.

	Type of Transportation			
Grade	**On Foot**	**By Car**	**By Bus**	**Total**
9	15	28	64	107
10	20	30	43	93
Total	35	58	107	200

5. Find the joint relative frequency of students surveyed who walk to
   school and are in grade 9.   _____

6. Given grade level, is that person more or less likely to travel to school
   by bus? Explain your response.

   _____

   _____

   _____

Name _____ Date _____ Class_____

Relative Frequency and Probability
Practice and Problem Solving: C

The two-way frequency table below represents the results of a survey about men, women, and televised sports.

1. Complete the table.

	Like Televised Sports		
Gender	Yes	No	Total
Men	48		73
Women	43	9	
Total		34	125

In Exercise 2–5, write your answers as percents.

2. Find the joint relative frequency of men surveyed who like televised sports. _____

3. Find the marginal relative frequency of people surveyed who like televised sports. _____

4. Given someone is male, is that person more or less likely to like televised sports? Explain.

_____

_____

5. Given someone likes televised sports, is that person more or less likely to be male? Explain your response.

_____

_____

The two-way frequency table below represents the results of a survey about ways people get to the movies.

6. Complete the table.

	Type of Transportation			
Age	On Foot	By Car	By Bus	Total
Adult	15	28	64	
Child		30	43	93
Total	35		107	

7. Find the joint relative frequency of people surveyed who walk to the movies and are adults. _____

8. Given that a person is an adult, is that person more or less likely to travel to the movies by bus? What about if the person is a child? Explain your response.

_____

_____

_____

Name _____ Date _____ Class_____

Measures of Center and Spread
Practice and Problem Solving: A/B

Find the mean, median, and range for each data set.

1. 18, 24, 26, 30

    Mean: _____

    Median: _____

    Range: _____

2. 5, 5, 9, 11, 13

    Mean: _____

    Median: _____

    Range: _____

3. 72, 91, 93, 89, 77, 82

    Mean: _____

    Median: _____

    Range: _____

4. 1.2, 0.4, 1.2, 2.4, 1.7, 1.6, 0.9, 1.0

    Mean: _____

    Median: _____

    Range: _____

The data sets below show the ages of the members of two clubs. Use the data for 5–9.

        Club A: 42, 38, 40, 34, 35, 48, 38, 45
        Club B: 22, 44, 43, 63, 22, 27, 58, 65

5. Find the mean, median, range, and interquartile range for Club A.

    _____

6. Find the mean, median, range, and interquartile range for Club B.

    _____

7. Find the standard deviation for each club. Round to the nearest tenth.

    _____

8. Use your statistics to compare the ages and the spread of ages on the two clubs.

    _____

    _____

    _____

9. Members of Club A claim that they have the "younger" club. Members of Club B make the same claim. Explain how that could happen.

    _____

    _____

Name _____ Date _____ Class_____

Measures of Center and Spread
Practice and Problem Solving: C

The data sets below show the price that a homeowner paid, per therm, for natural gas during each of the first ten months of 2011 and 2012. Use the data for 1–4.

2011: $1.59, $1.72, $1.71, $1.86, $2.32, $2.54, $2.45, $2.80, $2.38, $2.25
2012: $1.57, $1.61, $1.96, $1.71, $1.98, $2.17, $2.51, $2.44, $2.52, $2.10

1. Find the mean, median, range, and interquartile range for 2011.

_____

2. Find the mean, median, range, and interquartile range for 2012.

_____

3. Find the standard deviation for each year. Round to the nearest hundredth.

_____

4. Use your statistics to compare the overall trend in prices for the two years.

_____

_____

_____

Solve.

5. To earn an exemption from the final exam, Aaron needs his mean test score to be 92 or greater. If Aaron scored 90, 96, 87, and 90 on the first four tests and he has one test still to take, what is the lowest he can score and still earn an exemption?

_____

6. A, B, and C are positive integers with $A < B < C$. The mean of A, B, and C is 25, and their median is 10. Find all possible values for C.

_____

7. A teacher gave a test to 24 students and recorded the scores as a data set. Afterward, the teacher realized that the total number of points on the test added up to 96 instead of 100. To correct this, she added four points to each student's score. How did the mean, median, range, interquartile range, and standard deviation change from the original data set of scores when she added four points to each score?

_____

Data Distributions and Outliers

Practice and Problem Solving: A/B

For each data set, determine if 100 is an outlier. Explain why or why not.

1. 60, 68, 100, 70, 78, 80, 82, 88

_____

_____

2. 70, 75, 77, 78, 100, 80, 82, 88

_____

_____

The table below shows a major league baseball player's season home run totals for the first 14 years of his career. Use the data for Problems 3–8.

Season	1	2	3	4	5	6	7	8	9	10	11	12	13	14
Home Runs	18	22	21	28	30	29	32	40	33	34	28	29	22	20

3. Find the mean and median.

_____

4. Find the range and interquartile range.

_____

5. Make a dot plot for the data.

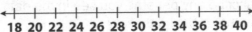

6. Examine the dot plot. Do you think any of the season home run totals are outliers? Then test for any possible outliers.

_____

_____

7. The player wants to predict how many home runs he will hit in his 15th season. Could he use the table or the dot plot to help him predict? Explain your reasoning.

_____

_____

_____

8. Suppose the player hits 10 home runs in his 15th season. Which of the statistics from Problems 3 and 4 would change?

_____

Name _____ Date _____ Class_____

Data Distributions and Outliers
Practice and Problem Solving: C

For each data set, determine if 100 is an outlier. Explain why or why not.

1. 90, 56, 78, 82, 75, 68, 88, 100, 75

2. 123, 111, 122, 100, 109, 117, 125, 121, 130

_____

_____

The table below shows the age of 20 presidents of the United States upon first taking office. Use the data for Problems 3–8.

54	42	51	56	55	51	54	51	60	62
43	55	56	61	52	69	64	46	54	47

3. Find the mean and median.

4. Find the range and interquartile range.

_____

_____

5. Make a dot plot for the data.

6. Examine the dot plot. Describe any patterns you see in the data. Could these patterns be seen in the original data set?

_____

_____

_____

7. Examine the dot plot. Test for any possible outliers.

_____

_____

_____

8. The most recent president of the United States not included in the data set above was Grover Cleveland, who took office on March 4, 1893. Based on your work so far, make an educated guess as to his age that day. Explain your reasoning. Then find his age.

_____

LESSON
9-3

Histograms and Box Plots

Practice and Problem Solving: A/B

Solve each problem.

1. The number of calls per day to a fire and rescue service for three weeks is given below. Use the data to complete the frequency table.

Calls for Service
5 17 2 12 0 6 3 8 15 1 4
19 16 8 2   11 13 18 3 10 6

Fire and Rescue Service	
Number of Calls	**Frequency**
0–3	
4–7	
8–11	
12–15	
16–19	

2. Use the frequency table in Exercise 1 to make a histogram with a title and axis labels.

3. Which intervals have the same frequency?

_____

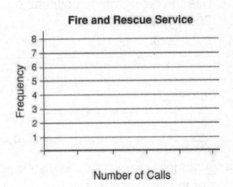

4. Use the histogram to estimate the mean. Then compare your answer with the actual mean, found by using the original data.

_____

_____

Use the box plot for Problems 5–7.

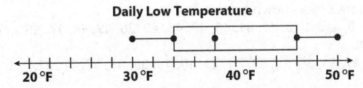

5. Find the median temperature.

_____

6. Find the range.

_____

7. Determine whether the temperature of 50 °F is an outlier.

_____

_____

_____

Histograms and Box Plots

Practice and Problem Solving: C

The histogram below shows the population distribution, by age, for the city of Somerville. Use the histogram to solve the problems that follow.

1. What is the approximate total population of the city?

   _____

2. Which age intervals have approximately the same total population?

   _____

3. Use the histogram to estimate the mean age. Show your work.

   _____

   _____

   _____

   _____

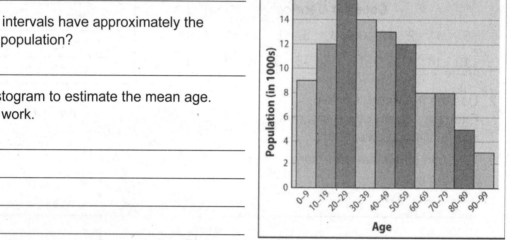

4. A student claims that the distribution is roughly symmetric. Do you agree? Why or why not?

   _____

   _____

Use the data for Problems 5–7. Harmon Killebrew and Willie Mays were two of baseball's all-time greatest home run hitters. Their season home run totals are shown below.
Harmon Killebrew: 0, 4, 5, 2, 0, 42, 31, 46, 48, 45, 49, 25, 39, 44, 17, 49, 41, 28, 26, 5, 13, 14
Willie Mays: 20, 4, 41, 51, 36, 35, 29, 34, 29, 40, 49, 38, 47, 52, 37, 22, 23, 13, 28, 18, 8, 6

5. Make a double box plot for Killebrew and Mays.

   ⟵————————————————⟶

6. Find mean and median season home run totals for Killebrew and Mays.

   _____

Normal Distributions
Practice and Problem Solving: A/B

A collection of data follows a normal distribution. Find the percent of the data that falls within the indicated range of the mean.

1. one standard deviation of the mean

_____

2. three standard deviations of the mean

_____

3. two standard deviations above the mean

_____

4. one standard deviation below the mean

_____

The amount of cereal in a carton is listed as 18 ounces. The cartons are filled by a machine, and the amount filled follows a normal distribution with mean of 18 ounces and standard deviation of 0.2 ounce. Use this information for 5–7.

5. Find the probability that a carton of cereal contains less than its listed amount.

_____

6. Find the probability that a carton of cereal contains between 18 ounces and 18.4 ounces.

_____

7. Find the probability that a carton of cereal contains between 17.6 ounces and 18.2 ounces.

_____

Suppose the manufacturer of the cereal above is concerned about your answer to Problem 5. A decision is made to leave the amount listed on the carton as 18 ounces while increasing the mean amount filled by the machine to 18.4 ounces. The standard deviation remains the same. Use this information for 8–11.

8. Find the probability that a carton contains less than its listed amount.

_____

9. Find the probability that a carton contains more than its listed amount.

_____

10. Find the probability that a carton now contains more than 18.2 ounces.

_____

11. Find the probability that a carton is more than 0.2 ounce under the weight listed on the carton.

_____

Name _____ Date _____ Class_____

Normal Distributions
Practice and Problem Solving: C

When a fair coin is tossed, it has a probability *p* of 0.5 that it will land showing Heads. If the coin is tossed *n* times, it can land showing Heads anywhere from 0 to *n* times.

1. Find the probability that a fair coin tossed *n* times will never land showing Heads. Evaluate for *n* = 5 and write as a percent.

   _____

2. Suppose a fair coin is tossed 1000 times. If you had to predict the number of times it will land showing Heads, what would your prediction be? Justify your answer.

   _____

The number of Heads obtained when a coin is tossed *n* times obeys a probability rule called the Binomial Distribution. For large *n*, this rule can be approximated using a normal distribution. In the case of a fair coin, the mean is 0.5*n* and the standard deviation is $0.5\sqrt{n}$. Use the normal distribution to estimate the following probabilities.

3. The probability that a fair coin tossed 100 times lands showing Heads between 45 and 55 times

   _____

4. The probability that a fair coin tossed 100 times lands showing Heads fewer than 45 times

   _____

5. The probability that a fair coin tossed 100 times lands showing Heads more than 65 times

   _____

6. The probability that a fair coin tossed 2500 times lands showing Heads between 1200 and 1300 times

   _____

Solve.

7. A coin is tossed 400 times as part of an experiment and lands showing Heads 221 times. A student concludes that this is not a fair coin. What do you think? Justify your reasoning.

   _____

   _____

   _____

LESSON 10-1

Scatter Plots and Trend Lines
Practice and Problem Solving: A/B

Graph a scatter plot and find the correlation.

1. The table shows the number of juice drinks sold at
   a small restaurant from 11:00 am to 1:00 pm.
   Graph a scatter plot using the given data.

Time	11:00	11:30	12:00	12:30	1:00
Number of Drinks	20	29	34	49	44

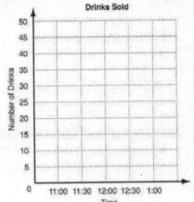

2. Name the two variables. _____

3. Write *positive*, *negative*, or *none* to describe the correlation
   illustrated by the scatter plot you drew in problem 1. Estimate
   the value of the correlation coefficient, *r*. Indicate whether *r* is
   closer to −1, −0.5, 0, 0.5, or 1.

   _____

**A city collected data on the amount of ice cream sold in the city each
day and the amount of suntan lotion sold at a nearby beach each day.**

4. Do you think there is causation between the city's two variables? If so,
   how? If not, is there a third variable involved? Explain.

   _____

Solve.

5. The number of snowboarders and skiers at a resort per day and the
   amount of new snow the resort reported that morning are shown in
   the table.

Amount of New Snow (in inches)	2	4	6	8	10
Number of Snowsliders	1146	1556	1976	2395	2490

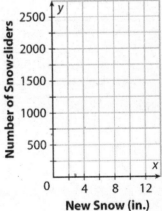

   a. Make a scatterplot of the data.

   b. Draw a line of fit on the graph above and find the equation

      for the linear model. _____

   c. If the resort reports 15 inches of new snow, how many skiers and
      snowboarders would you expect to be at the resort that day?

   _____

Scatter Plots and Trend Lines

LESSON 10-1

Practice and Problem Solving: C

Graph a scatter plot and find the correlation.

1. A biologist in a laboratory comes up with the following data points. Make a scatter plot using the data in the table.

x	2	6	9	14	16	21	25	28
y	3	7	15	33	38	35	40	41

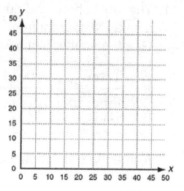

2. Draw a line of fit on the graph and find the equation for the liner model. Estimate the correlation coefficient, *r* (choose 1, 0.5, 0, –0.5, or –1).

_____   _____

3. Use a graphing calculator to find the equation for the line of best fit for the data presented in the table above. Use a graphing calculator to find the correlation coefficient, *r*.

_____   _____

4. Compare the results you found in step 3, using a graphing calculator, to those you found in step 2, estimating. The calculator provides a line of BEST fit, while the line you drew by hand is called a line of fit. Explain the difference.

_____

_____

_____

LESSON 10-2 Fitting a Linear Model to Data

Practice and Problem Solving: A/B

The table below lists the ages and heights of 10 children. Use the data for 1–5.

A, age in years	2	3	3	4	4	4	5	5	5	6
H, height in inches	30	33	34	37	35	38	40	42	43	42

1. Draw a scatter plot and line of fit for the data.

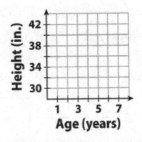

2. A student fit the line $H = 3.5A + 23$ to the data. Graph the student's line above. Then calculate the student's predicted values and residuals.

A, age in years	2	3	3	4	4	4	5	5	5	6
H, height in inches	30	33	34	37	35	38	40	42	43	42
Predicted Values										
Residuals										

3. Use the graph below to make a residual plot.

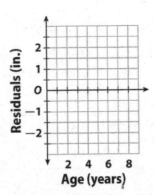

4. Use your residual plot to discuss how well the student's line fits the data.

_____

_____

5. Use the student's line to predict the height of a 20-year-old man. Discuss the reasonableness of the result.

_____

_____

Name _____ Date _____ Class_____

Fitting a Linear Model to Data

Practice and Problem Solving: C

Use the scatter plot, fitted line, and residual plot for 1–5.

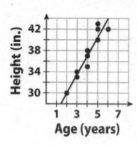

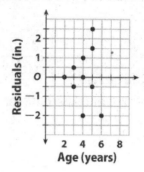

1. Find the equation of the line of fit shown above.

   _____

2. Use the line of fit to predict the height of a 20-year old man. Discuss
   the suitability of the linear model for extrapolation in this case.

   _____

   _____

3. Examine the residual plot. Does the distribution seem suitable?
   Discuss any issues you see.

   _____

   _____

4. The data for the scatter plot is shown in the first two rows of the table
   below. Complete the next two rows of the table.

A	2	3	3	4	4	4	5	5	5	6
H	30	33	34	37	35	38	40	42	43	42
AH										
A^2										

5. The row sums in the table above can be used to find a line of fit. This
   line is called the least-squares line of best fit. Use these formulas to
   find the slope and y-intercept of that line:

   _____

$$m = \frac{10 \cdot \text{sum}(AH) - \text{sum}(A) \cdot \text{sum}(H)}{10 \cdot \text{sum}(A^2) - (\text{sum}(A))^2}$$

   _____

$$b = \frac{\text{sum}(H) \cdot \text{sum}(A^2) - \text{sum}(A) \cdot \text{sum}(AH)}{10 \cdot \text{sum}(A^2) - (\text{sum}(A))^2}$$

   _____

LESSON 11-1

Solving Linear Systems by Graphing

Practice and Problem Solving: A/B

Tell the number of solutions for each system of two linear equations and state if the system is consistent or inconsistent and dependent or independent.

1.

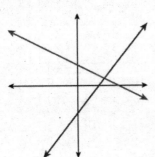

_____

_____

_____

2.

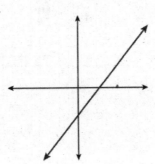

_____

_____

_____

3.

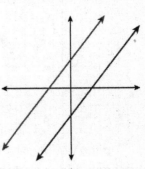

_____

_____

_____

Solve each system of linear equations by graphing.

4. $\begin{cases} x + y = 3 \\ -x + y = 1 \end{cases}$

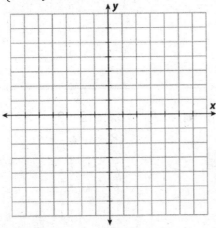

solution: _____

5. $\begin{cases} 6x + 3y = 12 \\ 8x + 4y = 24 \end{cases}$

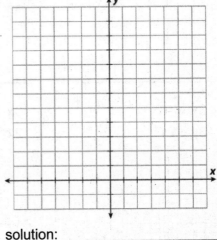

solution: _____

6. Jill babysits and earns y dollars at a rate of $8 per hour plus a $5 transportation fee. Samantha babysits and earns $2y$ dollars at $16 per hour plus a $10 transportation fee. Write a system of equations and graph to determine the number of hours each needs to babysit to earn the same amount of money.

_____

_____

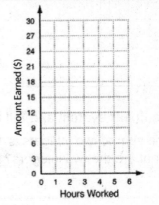

LESSON 11-1

Solving Linear Systems by Graphing

Practice and Problem Solving: C

Draw a graph of a system of linear equations that is:

1. consistent and independent 2. consistent and dependent 3. inconsistent

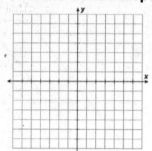
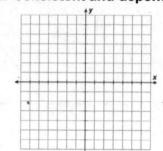
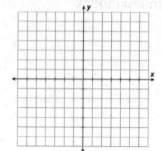

Solve each linear system by graphing. State if there is no solution or an infinite number of solutions.

4. $\begin{cases} 4x + 3y = 9 \\ 2x + y = 4 \end{cases}$

5. $\begin{cases} 4x - 5y = 20 \\ 8x - 12 = 10y \end{cases}$

6. $\begin{cases} x + 3y = 6 \\ 3x + 9y = 18 \end{cases}$

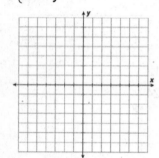
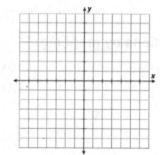
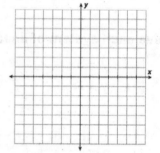

_____   _____   _____

7. $\begin{cases} x - 3y = -6 \\ x - 3y = 21 \end{cases}$

8. $\begin{cases} 3x + y = 4 \\ 2x - 2y = 8 \end{cases}$

9. $\begin{cases} 6x + 12 = 2y \\ 18 - 3y = -9x \end{cases}$

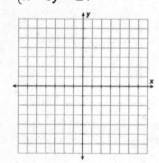
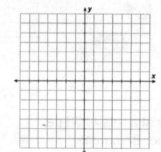
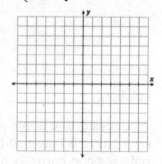

_____   _____   _____

Write a linear system and tell how to solve by graphing.

10. The sum of two integers is 12 and the difference of the two integers is 6.
    What are the two integers?

_____

LESSON 11-2

Solving Linear Systems by Substitution

Practice and Problem Solving: A/B

Solve each system by substitution. Check your answer.

1. $\begin{cases} y = x - 2 \\ y = 4x + 1 \end{cases}$

_____

2. $\begin{cases} y = x - 4 \\ y = -x + 2 \end{cases}$

_____

3. $\begin{cases} y = 3x + 1 \\ y = 5x - 3 \end{cases}$

_____

4. $\begin{cases} 2x - y = 6 \\ x + y = -3 \end{cases}$

_____

5. $\begin{cases} 2x + y = 8 \\ y = x - 7 \end{cases}$

_____

6. $\begin{cases} 2x + 3y = 0 \\ x + 2y = -1 \end{cases}$

_____

7. $\begin{cases} 3x - 2y = 7 \\ x + 3y = -5 \end{cases}$

_____

8. $\begin{cases} -2x + y = 0 \\ 5x + 3y = -11 \end{cases}$

_____

9. $\begin{cases} \dfrac{1}{2}x + \dfrac{1}{3}y = 5 \\ \dfrac{1}{4}x + y = 10 \end{cases}$

_____

Write a system of equations to solve.

10. A woman's age is three years more than twice her son's age. The sum of their ages is 84. How old is the son?

_____

11. The length of a rectangle is three times its width. The perimeter of the rectangle is 100 inches. What are the dimensions of the rectangle?

_____

12. Benecio worked 40 hours at his two jobs last week. He earned $20 per hour at his weekday job and $18 per hour at his weekend job. He earned $770 in all. How many hours did he work at each job?

_____

13. Choose one of Exercises 1–9 and graph its solution.

Does the answer you found by substitution agree with the answer you got by graphing?

_____

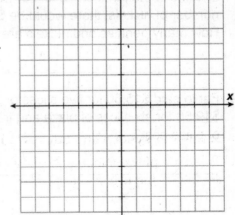

LESSON 11-2

Solving Linear Systems by Substitution

Practice and Problem Solving: C

Solve each system by substitution. Check your answer.

1. $\begin{cases} 4x - 9y = 1 \\ 2x + y = -5 \end{cases}$

2. $\begin{cases} \dfrac{1}{2}x + y = 2 \\ \dfrac{2}{3}x - \dfrac{1}{4}y = 28 \end{cases}$

3. $\begin{cases} 2x + 4y = 1 \\ x + 6y = 1 \end{cases}$

_____   _____   _____

Write a system of equations to solve.

4. Aaron is three times as old as his son. In ten years, Aaron will be twice as old as his son. How old is Aaron now?

_____

5. Kitara has 100 quarters and dimes. Their total value is $19. How many of each coin does Kitara have?

_____

6. A cleaning company charges a fixed amount for a house call and a second amount for each room it cleans. The total cost to clean six rooms is $250 and the total cost to clean eight rooms is $320. How much would this company charge to clean two rooms?

_____

7. Willie Mays and Mickey Mantle hit 88 home runs one season to lead their leagues. Mays hit 14 more home runs than Mantle that year. How many home runs did Willie Mays hit?

_____

8. Coco has a jar containing pennies and nickels. There is $9.20 worth of coins in the jar. If she could switch the number of pennies with the number of nickels, there would be $26.80 worth of coins in the jar. How many pennies and nickels are in the jar?

_____

9. Fabio paid $15.50 for five slices of pizza and two sodas. Liam paid $19.50 for six slices of pizza and three sodas. How much does a slice of pizza cost?

_____

LESSON 11-3 Solving Linear Systems by Adding or Subtracting
Practice and Problem Solving: A/B

Solve each system of linear equations by adding or subtracting.
Check your answer.

1. $x - 5y = 10$
   $2x + 5y = 5$

2. $x + y = -10$
   $5x + y = -2$

_____

_____

3. $4x + 10y = 2$
   $-4x + 8y = 16$

4. $-3x - 7y = 8$
   $3x - 2y = -44$

_____

_____

5. $-x + 4y = 15$
   $3x + 4y = 3$

6. $-4x + 11y = 5$
   $4x - 11y = -5$

_____

_____

7. $-x - y = 1$
   $-x + y = -1$

8. $3x - 5y = 60$
   $4x + 5y = -4$

_____

_____

Write a system of equations to solve.

9. A plumber charges an initial amount to make a house call plus an hourly rate for the time he is working. A 1-hour job costs $90 and a 3-hour job costs $210. What is the initial amount and the hourly rate that the plumber charges?

_____

10. A man and his three children spent $40 to attend a show. A second family of three children and their two parents spent $53 for the same show. How much does a child's ticket cost?

_____

Solving Linear Systems by Adding or Subtracting
Practice and Problem Solving: C

**Solve each system of linear equations by adding or subtracting.
Check your answer.**

1. $0.5x - 3y = 1$
   $1.5x + 3y = 9$

   _____

2. $2x + \dfrac{1}{2}y = 6$

   $2x + \dfrac{1}{4}y = 8$

   _____

3. $-4x + 7y = 11$
   $4x - 9y = -13$

   _____

4. $\dfrac{1}{3}x + y = 0$

   $\dfrac{2}{5}x + y = 5$

   _____

5. A theater charges $25 for adults and $15 for children. When the
   theater increases its prices next year, the price of a child's ticket will
   increase to $18 and the cost for the members of a dance club to attend
   the theater will increase from $450 to $480. Write and solve a system
   of equations to find how many adults are in the dance club.

   _____

6. Pearl solved a system of two linear equations. In the final step, she
   found herself writing "0 = 6." Pearl thought she had done something
   wrong, but she had not. Explain what occurred here and how the
   graphs of the two equations are related.

   _____

   _____

7. The equations $ax + by = c$ and $dx - by = e$ form a system of
   equations where a, b, c, d, and e are real numbers with $a \neq -d$. Solve
   the system for x.

   _____

   _____

Name _____ Date _____ Class _____

Solving Linear Systems by Multiplying First

Practice and Problem Solving: A/B

Solve each system of equations. Check your answer.

1. $\begin{cases} -3x - 4y = -2 \\ 6x + 4y = 3 \end{cases}$

2. $\begin{cases} 2x - 2y = 14 \\ x + 4y = -13 \end{cases}$

_____

3. $\begin{cases} y - x = 17 \\ 2y + 3x = -11 \end{cases}$

4. $\begin{cases} x + 6y = 1 \\ 2x - 3y = 32 \end{cases}$

_____

5. $\begin{cases} 3x + y = -15 \\ 2x - 3y = 23 \end{cases}$

6. $\begin{cases} 5x - 2y = -48 \\ 2x + 3y = -23 \end{cases}$

_____

Solve each system of equations. Check your answer by graphing.

7. $\begin{cases} 4x - 3y = -9 \\ 5x - y = 8 \end{cases}$

8. $\begin{cases} 3x - 3y = -1 \\ 12x - 2y = 16 \end{cases}$

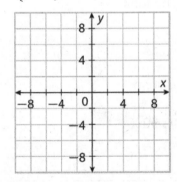

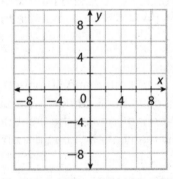

Solve.

9. Ten bagels and four muffins cost $13. Five bagels and eight muffins cost $14. What are the prices of a bagel and a muffin?

_____

10. John can service a television and a cable box in one hour. It took him four hours yesterday to service two televisions and ten cable boxes. How many minutes does John need to service a cable box?

_____

Solving Linear Systems by Multiplying First

Practice and Problem Solving: C

Solve each system of equations. Check your answer.

1. $-x + \frac{1}{2}y = 8$

   $3x - 4y = -39$

2. $\frac{1}{3}x + \frac{1}{4}y = 5$

   $\frac{1}{6}x - \frac{2}{3}y = 31$

3. $5x = 3y + 18$

   $3x + 5y = 4$

4. $0.25x - 6y = 17$

   $0.07x + 0.4y = -2$

Write a system of equations to solve.

5. Travis has $60 in dimes and quarters. If he could switch the numbers of dimes with the number of quarters, he would have $87. How many of each coin does Travis have?

6. The total cost of a bus ride and a ferry ride is $8.00. In one month, bus fare will increase by 10% and ferry fare will increase by 25%. The total cost will then be $9.25. How much is the current bus fare?

7. A truckload of 10-pound and 50-pound bags of fertilizer weighs 9000 pounds. A second truck carries twice as many 10-pound bags and half as many 50-pound bags as the first truck. That load also weighs 9000 pounds. How many of each bag are on the first truck?

8. The hundreds digit and the ones digit of a three-digit number are the same. The sum of its three digits is 16. If the tens digit and the ones digit are exchanged, the number increases by 45. What is the number?

Name _____ Date _____ Class _____

Creating Systems of Linear Equations
12-1
Practice and Problem Solving: A/B

Write and solve a system of equations for each situation.

1. One week Beth bought 3 apples and 8 pears for $14.50. The next week she bought 6 apples and 4 pears and paid $14. Find the cost of 1 apple and the cost of 1 pear.

   _____

2. Brian bought beverages for his coworkers. One day he bought 3 lemonades and 4 iced teas for $12.00. The next day he bought 5 lemonades and 2 iced teas for $11.50. Find the cost of 1 lemonade and 1 iced tea, to the nearest cent.

   _____

Two campgrounds rent a campsite for one night according to the following table. Use the table for 3–5.

Number of campers	Sunnyside Campground	Green Mountain Campground
1	$58	$40
2	$66	$50
3	$74	$60
4	$82	$70

3. Write the equation for the rate charged by Sunnyside Campground.

   _____

4. Write the equation for the rate charged by Green Mountain.

   _____

5. Solve the system of the equations you found in Problems 3 and 4. For how many campers do the campgrounds charge the same rate? What is the rate charged for that number of campers?

   _____

Use the graph for 6–8.

6. Write the functions represented by the graph. _____

7. What does each function represent? What does the variable represent?

   _____

8. Solve the system of equations. Is the intersection point shown on the graph correct?

   _____

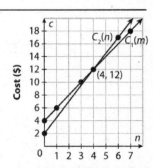

Name _____ Date _____ Class_____

 LESSON 12-1

Creating Systems of Linear Equations
Practice and Problem Solving: C

Use the graph for 1–3.

1. Write the equation for the line of the graph.

2. Develop a real-world scenario that could be solved by this equation. Examples may be "the number of bales of hay needed to feed 4 elephants," or "the cost of 6 sandwiches and 4 iced teas." Record your idea:

    _____

    _____

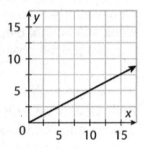

3. Select one point on the line. Write two more equations that also have this point as a solution. Graph the two new equations.

    Let *x* = _____   Let *y* = _____

    equations: _____   _____

4. Make a chart of the information another student could use to write the equations and find the solution for all three equations. What information will you need to show? Label the columns and rows according to the scenario you chose.

5. Write your own problem, asking students to find the equations from the chart above. Write a complete solution for your problem on another sheet of paper.

    _____

    _____

    _____

    _____

Name _____ Date _____ Class_____

Graphing Systems of Linear Inequalities
Practice and Problem Solving: A/B

Tell whether the ordered pair is a solution of the given system.

1. $(2, -2)$; $\begin{cases} y < x - 3 \\ y > -x + 1 \end{cases}$

2. $(2, 5)$; $\begin{cases} y > 2x \\ y \geq x + 2 \end{cases}$

3. $(1, 3)$; $\begin{cases} y \leq x + 2 \\ y > 4x - 1 \end{cases}$

_____   _____   _____

Graph the system of linear inequalities. a. Give two ordered pairs that are solutions. b. Give two ordered pairs that are not solutions.

4. $\begin{cases} y \leq x + 4 \\ y \geq -2x \end{cases}$

5. $\begin{cases} y \leq \dfrac{1}{2}x + 1 \\ x + y < 3 \end{cases}$

6. $\begin{cases} y > x - 4 \\ y < x + 2 \end{cases}$

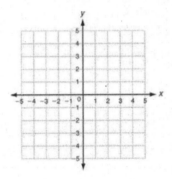
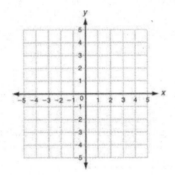
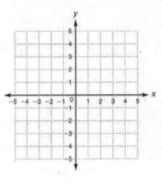

a. _____   a. _____   a. _____

b. _____   b. _____   b. _____

7. Charlene makes $10 per hour babysitting and $5 per hour gardening. She wants to make at least $80 a week, but can work no more than 12 hours a week.

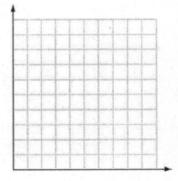

   a. Write a system of linear equations.

   _____

   b. Graph the solutions of the system.

   c. Describe all the possible combinations of hours that Charlene could work at each job.

   _____

   _____

   d. List two possible combinations. _____

   _____

LESSON
12-2
Graphing Systems of Linear Inequalities
Practice and Problem Solving: C

The coordinate grid below shows a system of two linear equations. For each problem, state the system of inequalities that generates the region indicated as its solution. Write the inequalities in terms of *y*.

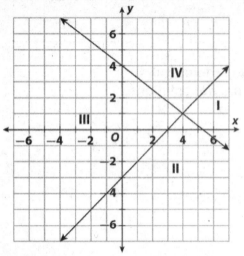

1. Region I

2. Region II

3. Region III

4. Region IV

_____   _____   _____   _____

_____   _____   _____   _____

The inequalities *x* ≥ –5, *y* ≥ –5, *x* + *y* ≤ 1, and 2*x* – *y* ≤ 5 form a system. Use this system for Problems 5–7.

5. Graph the system.

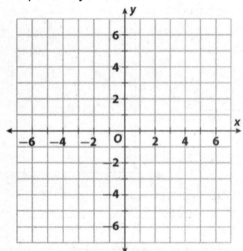

6. Describe geometrically the shaded region that represents the system's solution. Identify the vertices of that region.

7. Each square on the coordinate grid has an area of 1 square unit. Find the area of the shaded region in your graph above. Show your method fully.

Name _____ Date _____ Class_____

Modeling with Linear Systems
Practice and Problem Solving: A/B

Write a system of equations to solve each problem.

1. For a small party of 12 people, the caterer offered a choice of a steak dinner for $12.00 per meal or a chicken dinner for $10.50 per meal. The final cost for the meals was $138.00. How many of each meal was ordered?

   Equations: _____

   Solution: _____

2. A clubhouse was furnished with a total of 9 couches and love seats so that all 23 members of the club could be seated at once. Each couch seats 3 people and each love seat seats 2 people. How many couches and how many love seats are in the clubhouse?

   Equations: _____

   Solution: _____

3. A small art museum charges $5 for an adult ticket and $3 for a student ticket. At the end of the day, the museum had sold 89 tickets and made $371. How many student tickets and how many adult tickets were sold?

   Equations: _____

   Solution: _____

4. Cassie has a total of 110 coins in her piggy bank. All the coins are quarters and dimes. The coins have a total value of $20.30. How many quarters and how many dimes are in the piggy bank?

   Equations: _____

   Solution: _____

Write a system of inequalities and graph them to solve the problem.

5. Jack is buying tables and chairs for his deck party. Tables cost $25 and chairs cost $15. He plans to spend no more than $285 and buy at least 16 items. Show and describe the solution set, and suggest a reasonable solution to the problem.

   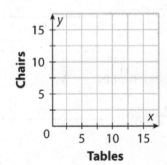

   Equations: _____

   Solution: _____

LESSON 12-3

Modeling with Linear Systems
Practice and Problem Solving: C

Write and solve a system of linear equations for each problem.
Solve each problem using two different methods.

1. A flower shop displays 41 vases for sale throughout the shop. Large vases cost $22 each and small vases cost $14 each. The vases on display have a combined value of $710. How many of each size of vase are on display?

   Equations: _____

   _____

   Solution: _____

2. Some members of the ski club and some faculty chaperones are on an overnight ski trip. They reserved one $120 hotel room for every 4 students and one $90 hotel room for every 2 faculty chaperones, or 27 rooms in all for $2880. How many students and how many faculty chaperones are on the trip?

   Equations: _____

   _____

   Solution: _____

Write a system of inequalities and graph them to solve the problem.

3. Lane is buying fish for his aquarium. Tetras cost $5 each and cichlids cost $19 each. Lane would like to have at least 8 fish in all, but he can spend no more than $100. Describe the solution set and give a reasonable solution.

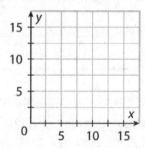

   Equations: _____

   _____

   Solution set: _____

   Solution: _____

LESSON 13-1

Understanding Piecewise-Defined Functions

Practice and Problem Solving: A/B

Graph each piecewise-defined function.

1. $f(x) = \begin{cases} 0.5x - 1.5 & x < -1 \\ x + 1 & -1 \le x \le 3 \\ 4 & x > 3 \end{cases}$

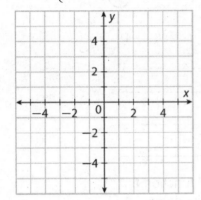

2. $f(x) = \begin{cases} -4x - 16 & x < -3 \\ 0.5x - 4.5 & -3 \le x < 3 \\ -2 & x \ge 3 \end{cases}$

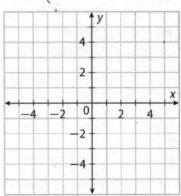

Write equations to complete the definition of each function.

3.

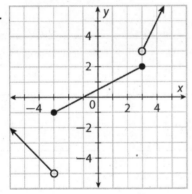

_____

4.

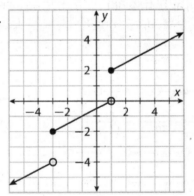

_____

5. The graph at the right shows shipping cost as a function of purchase amount.

Find the shipping cost for each purchase amount.

purchase amount: $8.49 _____

purchase amount: $20.00 _____

purchase amount: $89.50 _____

purchase amount: $40.01 _____

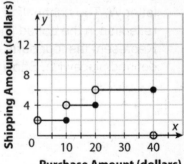

LESSON
13-1
Understanding Piecewise-Defined Functions
Practice and Problem Solving: C

1. The incomplete piecewise-defined function at the right is represented by this graph.

   Find real numbers *a* and *c* to complete the definition of *f*. Show your work.

   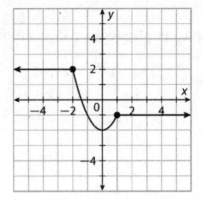

   $$f(x) = \begin{cases} 2 & x < -2 \\ ax^2 + c & -2 \le x \le 1 \\ -1 & x > 1 \end{cases}$$

   _____

   _____

   _____

2. The graph at the left below represents a piecewise-defined function *f*. It is defined for all real numbers *x*. The pattern shown continues as suggested both to the left and to the right indefinitely. Which is greater, *f*(48) or *f*(30)? Explain.

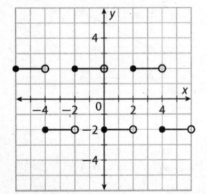

   _____

   _____

   _____

   _____

3. The diagram at the right shows the left half of the letter W. The right half of the letter is formed by reflection in the dotted line.
   Represent the four parts of the letter as a function *f* defined piecewise. Show your work.

   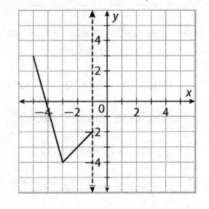

   _____

   _____

   _____

   _____

LESSON 13-2 Absolute Value Functions and Transformations

Practice and Problem Solving: A/B

Create a table of values for *f(x)*, graph the function, and tell the domain and range.

1. $f(x) = |x - 3| + 2$

x	f(x)

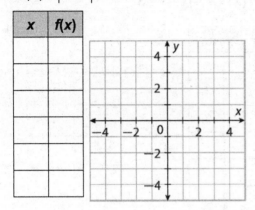

_____

2. $f(x) = 2|x + 1| - 2$

x	f(x)

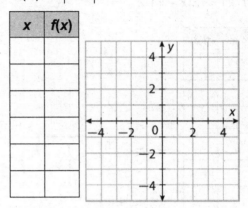

_____

Write an equation for each absolute value function whose graph is shown.

3.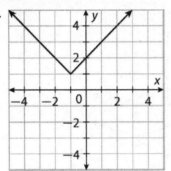

_____

4.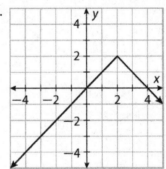

_____

Solve.

5. A machine is used to fill bags with sand. The average weight of a bag filled with sand is 22.3 pounds. Write an absolute value function describing the difference between the weight of an average bag of sand and a bag of sand with an unknown weight.

_____

Name _____ Date _____ Class_____

Absolute Value Functions and Transformations
Practice and Problem Solving: C

Create a table of values for *f(x)*, graph the function, and tell the domain and range.

1. $f(x) = -2|x - 1| + 2$

x	f(x)

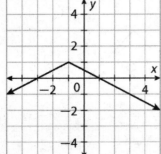

_____

2. $f(x) = -\dfrac{1}{2}|x + 1| + 3$

x	f(x)

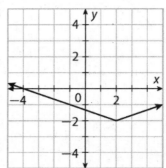

_____

Write an equation for each absolute value function whose graph is shown.

3.

_____

4.

_____

Solve.

5. Suppose you plan to ride your bicycle from Portland, Oregon, to Seattle, Washington, and back to Portland. The distance between Portland and Seattle is 175 miles. You plan to ride 25 miles each day. Write an absolute value function *d(x)*, where *x* is the number of days into the ride, that describes your distance from Portland and use your function to determine the number of days it will take to complete your ride.

_____

LESSON 13-3 Solving Absolute Value Equations

Practice and Problem Solving: A/B

Solve.

1. How many solutions does the equation $|x + 7| = 1$ have? _____

2. How many solutions does the equation $|x + 7| = 0$ have? _____

3. How many solutions does the equation $|x + 7| = -1$ have? _____

Solve each equation algebraically.

4. $|x| = 12$

5. $|x| = \dfrac{1}{2}$

6. $|x| - 6 = 4$

_____ _____ _____

7. $5 + |x| = 14$

8. $3|x| = 24$

9. $|x + 3| = 10$

_____ _____ _____

Solve each equation graphically.

10. $|x - 1| = 2$

11. $4|x - 5| = 12$

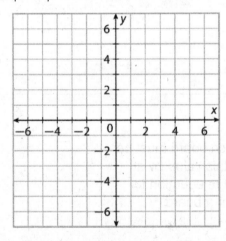 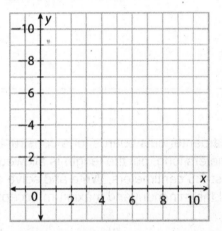

_____ _____

Leticia sets the thermostat in her apartment to 68 degrees. The actual temperature in her apartment can vary from this by as much as 3.5 degrees.

12. Write an absolute-value equation that you can

   use to find the minimum and maximum temperature. _____

13. Solve the equation to find the minimum and

   maximum temperature. _____

LESSON
13-3

Solving Absolute Value Equations

Practice and Problem Solving: C

Solve each equation algebraically.

1. $|x| + 6 = -4$

2. $-9|x| = -63$

3. $|x + 11| = 0$

_____

_____

_____

4. $\left|x - \dfrac{1}{2}\right| = 2$

5. $3|x - 1| = -15$

6. $|x - 1| - 1.4 = 6.2$

_____

_____

_____

Solve each equation graphically.

7. $\dfrac{|4x - 1|}{2} = 1$

8. $-3|5x - 2| = -12$

_____

_____

Solve.

9. A carpenter cuts boards for a construction project. Each board must be 3 meters long, but the length is allowed to differ from this value by at most 0.5 centimeters. Write and solve an absolute-value equation to find the minimum and maximum acceptable lengths for a board.

_____

_____

10. The owner of a butcher shop keeps the shop's freezer at –5 °C. It is acceptable for the temperature to differ from this value by 1.5 °C. Write and solve an absolute-value equation to find the minimum and maximum acceptable temperatures.

_____

_____

Name _____ Date _____ Class _____

Solving Absolute Value Inequalities
Practice and Problem Solving: A/B

Solve each inequality and graph the solutions.

1. $|x| - 2 \le 3$

_____

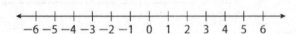

2. $|x + 1| + 5 < 7$

_____

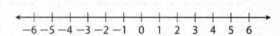

3. $3|x - 6| \le 9$

_____

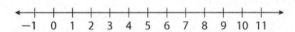

4. $|x + 3| - 1.5 < 2.5$

_____

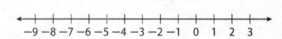

5. $|x| + 17 > 20$

_____

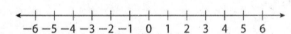

6. $|x - 6| - 7 > -3$

_____

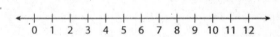

7. $\dfrac{1}{2}|x + 5| \ge 2$

_____

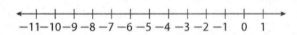

8. $2|x - 2| \ge 3$

_____

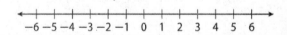

Solve.

9. The organizers of a drama club wanted to sell 350 tickets to their show. The actual sales were no more than 35 tickets from this goal. Write and solve an absolute-value inequality to find the range of the number of tickets that could have been sold.

_____

10. The temperature at noon in Los Angeles on a summer day was 88 °F. During the day, the temperature varied from this by as much as 7.5 °F. Write and solve an absolute-value inequality to find the range of possible temperatures for that day.

_____

**LESSON
13-4**

Solving Absolute Value Inequalities

Practice and Problem Solving: C

Solve each inequality and graph the solutions.

1. $|x| - 7 < -4$

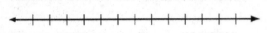

..2. $|x - 3| + 0.7 < 2.7$

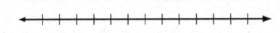

3. $\frac{1}{3}|x + 2| \le 1$

4. $|x - 5| - 3 > 1$

5. $|5x| \ge 15$

6. $\left|x + \frac{1}{2}\right| - 2 \ge 2$

7. $|x - 2| + 7 \ge 3$

8. $4|x - 6| \ge -8$

Solve.

9. The ideal temperature for a refrigerator is 36.5 °F. It is acceptable for the temperature to differ from this value by at most 1.5 °F. Write and solve an absolute-value inequality to find the range of acceptable temperatures.

_____

10. At a trout farm, most of the trout have a length of 23.5 cm. The length of some of the trout differs from this by as much as 2.1 cm. Write and solve an absolute-value inequality to find the range of lengths of the trout.

_____

11. Ben says that there is no solution for this absolute-value inequality. Is he correct? If not, solve the inequality. Explain how you know you are correct.

$$32 + \frac{|x - 7|}{13} < 7$$

_____

_____

_____

LESSON 14-1 **Understanding Rational Exponents and Radicals**

Practice and Problem Solving: A/B

Write the name of the property that is demonstrated by each equation.

1. $(2a)^4 = 16a^4$

2. $(3^6)^3 = 3^{18}$

_____   _____

Simplify each expression.

3. $8^{\frac{2}{3}}$

4. $1^{\frac{3}{5}}$

5. $9^{\frac{1}{2}}$

_____   _____   _____

6. $25^{\frac{3}{2}}$

7. $16^{\frac{5}{4}}$

8. $27^{\frac{1}{3}}$

_____   _____   _____

9. $81^{\frac{1}{4}} + 4^{\frac{1}{2}}$

10. $343^{\frac{2}{3}} \cdot 32^{\frac{2}{5}}$

11. $100^{-\frac{1}{2}}$

_____   _____   _____

Find the value of the expression for the value indicated.

12. $6a^{\frac{3}{4}}$ for $a = 16$

13. $c^{\frac{1}{2}} + c^{\frac{1}{3}}$ for $c = 64$

_____   _____

14. $\dfrac{m^{\frac{3}{5}}}{8}$ for $m = 32$

15. $0.5d^{\frac{5}{7}}$ for $d = 128$

_____   _____

Solve.

16. The equation $t = 0.25d^{\frac{1}{2}}$ can be used to find the number of seconds, t, that it takes an object to fall a distance of d feet. How long does it take an object to fall 64 feet?

_____

17. Show that $\left(16^{\frac{1}{4}}\right)^3$ and $\left(16^3\right)^{\frac{1}{4}}$ are equivalent.

_____

18. The surface area, S, of a cube with volume V can be found using the formula $S = 6V^{\frac{2}{3}}$. Find the surface area of a cube whose volume is 125 cubic inches.

_____

LESSON 14-1 Understanding Rational Exponents and Radicals

Practice and Problem Solving: C

Simplify each expression. Assume all variables represent positive numbers.

1. $27^{\frac{2}{3}} - 125^{\frac{1}{3}}$

2. $\left(a^4\right)^3$

3. $25^{-\frac{3}{2}}$

_____ _____ _____

4. $\left(16b^4\right)^{\frac{3}{4}}$

5. $4^{\frac{25}{2}} - 8^{\frac{25}{3}}$

6. $\left(n^{\frac{2}{3}}\right)^{\frac{3}{2}}$

_____ _____ _____

7. $512^{\frac{2}{3}} \cdot 100{,}000^{\frac{2}{5}}$

8. $\dfrac{k^{\frac{3}{4}}}{k^{\frac{1}{2}}}$

9. $\dfrac{\left(w^{-2}\right)^3}{w^{-8}}$

_____ _____ _____

Find the value of the expression for the value indicated.

10. $100m^{-2}$ for $m = 5$

11. $\left(81^a\right)^a$ for $a = \dfrac{1}{2}$

_____ _____

12. $\dfrac{27^x}{27^{-x}}$ for $x = \dfrac{2}{3}$

13. $\left(441^k + 784^k\right)^k$ for $k = \dfrac{1}{2}$

_____ _____

Solve.

14. Use the Quotient of Powers Property to explain why a^0 must equal
    1 for all positive values of a. *Hint*: Examine $\dfrac{a^2}{a^2}$.

_____

_____

15. Use your knowledge of fractional exponents to show that the following
    statement is true: *The square root of the cube root of a number equals
    the sixth root of that number.*

_____

_____

LESSON 14-2
Simplifying Expressions with Rational Exponents and Radicals
Practice and Problem Solving: A/B

Simplify each expression.

1. $\sqrt[5]{y^5}$

_____

2. $\sqrt{x^4 y^{12}}$

_____

3. $\sqrt[3]{a^6 b^3}$

_____

4. $\sqrt{25y^4}$

_____

5. $\sqrt[3]{x^6 y^9}$

_____

6. $\sqrt{(9y^2)^2}\ \sqrt{(9y^2)^2}$

_____

7. $\sqrt[5]{(32y^5)^3}$

_____

8. $(x^{\frac{1}{3}}y)^3 \sqrt{x^2 y^2}$

_____

9. $\sqrt[3]{(27y^3)^4}\ \sqrt[6]{(27y^3)^4}$

_____

10. $\sqrt[4]{(xy)^8}$

_____

11. $(x^{\frac{1}{2}})^4 \sqrt{x^6}$

_____

12. $\dfrac{(x^{\frac{1}{4}})^8}{\sqrt[3]{x^3}}$

_____

Solve.

13. Given a cube with volume V, you can use the formula $P = 4V^{\frac{1}{3}}$ to find the perimeter of one of the cube's square faces. Find the perimeter of a face of a cube that has volume 125 m³.

_____

14. The Beaufort Scale measures the intensity of tornadoes. For a tornado with Beaufort number B, the formula $v = 1.9B^{\frac{3}{2}}$ may be used to estimate the tornado's wind speed in miles per hour. Estimate the wind speed of a tornado with Beaufort number 9.

_____

15. At a factory that makes cylindrical cans, the formula $r = \left(\dfrac{V}{12}\right)^{\frac{1}{2}}$ is used to find the radius of a can with volume V. What is the radius of a can with a volume of 192 cm³?

_____

LESSON 14-2

Simplifying Expressions with Rational Exponents and Radicals
Practice and Problem Solving: C

Find a path from start to finish in the maze below. Each box that you pass through must have a value that is greater than or equal to the value in the previous box. You may only move horizontally or vertically to go from one box to the next.

START

$16^{\frac{1}{4}}$	$4^{\frac{1}{2}} - 27^{\frac{1}{3}}$	$0^{\frac{1}{5}}$	$1^{\frac{2}{3}} - 8^{\frac{1}{3}}$	$216^{\frac{2}{3}}$	$8^{\frac{1}{3}} + 9^{\frac{3}{2}}$
$36^{\frac{1}{2}} - 216^{\frac{1}{3}}$	$25^{\frac{1}{2}} - 32^{\frac{2}{5}}$	$9^{\frac{1}{2}} - 8^{\frac{1}{3}}$	$1^{\frac{3}{5}}$	$64^{\frac{1}{6}}$	$100^{\frac{1}{2}} + 27^{\frac{2}{3}}$
$1^{\frac{1}{2}} - 9^{\frac{3}{2}}$	$125^{\frac{2}{3}}$	$81^{\frac{3}{4}}$	$1000^{\frac{2}{3}}$	$16^{\frac{1}{2}} - 16^{\frac{1}{4}}$	$32^{\frac{1}{5}} + 0^{\frac{3}{4}}$
$512^{\frac{2}{9}}$	$9^{\frac{1}{2}} + 3^{\frac{4}{4}}$	$32^{\frac{2}{5}}$	$27^{\frac{1}{3}}$	$121^{0} + 1^{\frac{1}{2}}$	$9^{\frac{1}{2}} - 3^{0}$
$49^{\frac{1}{2}} + 0^{\frac{1}{2}}$	$16^{\frac{3}{4}}$	$16^{\frac{1}{4}} - 1^{\frac{3}{2}}$	$1024^{\frac{1}{10}}$	$81^{\frac{1}{4}} + 49^{\frac{1}{2}}$	$243^{\frac{4}{5}}$
$16^{\frac{3}{4}} + 32^{\frac{1}{5}}$	$100^{\frac{1}{2}}$	$625^{\frac{1}{4}}$	$128^{\frac{2}{7}}$	$144^{\frac{1}{2}} - 81^{\frac{1}{2}}$	$64^{\frac{1}{3}}$
$125^{\frac{1}{3}} - 2^{0}$	$81^{\frac{3}{4}} - 32^{\frac{4}{5}}$	$256^{\frac{1}{2}}$	$16^{\frac{3}{4}} + 4^{\frac{3}{2}}$	$64^{\frac{2}{3}}$	$32^{\frac{1}{5}} + 100^{\frac{1}{2}}$
$625^{\frac{1}{4}}$	$64^{\frac{5}{6}} - 125^{\frac{2}{3}}$	$243^{\frac{2}{5}}$	$125^{\frac{2}{3}}$	$128^{\frac{3}{7}}$	$243^{\frac{1}{5}}$

FINISH

LESSON 15-1

Understanding Geometric Sequences

Practice and Problem Solving: A/B

Find the common ratio *r* for each geometric sequence and use *r* to find the next three terms.

1. 3, 9, 27, 81, ...   *r* = _____

   Next three terms: _____

2. 972, 324, 108, 36, ...   *r* = _____

   Next three terms: _____

Complete.

3. The 11th term in a geometric sequence is 48 and the common ratio is 4.

   The 12th term is _____ and the 10th term is _____.

4. 7 and 105 are successive terms in a geometric sequence. The

   term following 105 is _____ .

Find the common difference *d* of the arithmetic sequence and write the next three terms.

5. 6, 11, 16, 21, ...   *d* = _____

   Next three terms: _____

6. 7, 4, 1, –2, ...   *d* = _____

   Next three terms: _____

Use the table to answer Exercise 7.

Bounce	Height
1	24
2	12
3	6

7. A ball is dropped from the top of a building.

   The table shows its height in feet above ground at the top of each bounce.

   What is the height of the ball at the top of bounce 5? _____

8. Tom's bank balances at the end of months 1, 2, and 3 are $1600,

   $1664, and $1730.56. What will Tom's balance be at the end of month 5? _____

9. Consider the geometric sequence 6, –18, 54.... Select all that apply.
   - A. The common ratio is 3.
   - B. The 6th term is –1458.
   - C. The 4th term is –3 times 54.
   - D. $6(-3)^{11}$ is smaller than $6(-3)^{10}$.

Find the indicated term by using the common ratio.

10. 108, –72, 48, ...; 5th term

   _____

LESSON 15-1 Understanding Geometric Sequences

Practice and Problem Solving: C

Find the common ratio *r* for each geometric sequence and use *r* to find the next three terms.

1. 4, 5, 6.25, ... $r =$ _____

   Next three terms: _____

2. 864, –288, 96, ... $r =$ _____

   Next three terms: _____

Complete.

3. The 11th term in a geometric sequence is 48 and the common ratio is –0.8.

   The 12th term is _____ and the 10th term is _____.

4. 8.5 and 11.9 are successive terms in a geometric sequence. The

   term following 11.9 is _____ .

Find the common difference *d* of the arithmetic sequence and write the next three terms.

5. 8, 17.6, 27.2, ... $d =$ _____

   Next three terms: _____

6. 4, –2.5, –9, ... $d =$ _____

   Next three terms: _____

Use the table to answer Exercise 7.

Bounce	Height
1	36
2	27
3	20.25

7. A ball is dropped from the top of a building.

   The table shows its height in feet above ground at the top of each bounce.

   To the nearest hundredth, what is the height of the ball at the top of bounce 5?

8. Lee's bank balances at the end of months 1, 2, and 3 are $1600, $1640, and $1681.

   What will Lee's balance be at the end of month 5? _____

9. Consider the geometric sequence –12, 19.2, –30.72.... Select all that apply.
   - A. The common ratio is –1.6.
   - B. The 5th term is 78.6432.
   - C. The 4th term is 1.6 times –30.72.
   - D. $-12(-1.6)^9$ is smaller than $-12(-1.6)^8$.

Find the indicated term by using the common ratio.

10. 108, –27, 6.75, ...; 5th term

   _____

LESSON 15-2 Constructing Geometric Sequences

Practice and Problem Solving: A/B

Complete.

1. Below are the first five terms of a geometric series. Fill in the bottom row by writing each term as the product of the first term and a power of the common ratio.

N	1	2	3	4	5
$f(n)$	3	12	48	192	768
$f(n)$					

The general rule is $f(n) =$ _____.

Each rule represents a geometric sequence. If the given rule is recursive, write it as an explicit rule. If the rule is explicit, write it as a recursive rule. Assume that $f(1)$ is the first term of the sequence.

2. $f(n) = 11(2)^{n-1}$

3. $f(1) = 2.5; f(n) = f(n-1) \bullet 3.5$ for $n \geq 2$

_____

_____

4. $f(1) = 27; f(n) = f(n-1) \bullet \dfrac{1}{3}$ for $n \geq 2$

5. $f(n) = -4(0.5)^{n-1}$

_____

_____

Write an explicit rule for each geometric sequence based on the given terms from the sequence. Assume that the common ratio r is positive.

6. $a_1 = 90$ and $a_2 = 360$

7. $a_1 = 16$ and $a_3 = 4$

_____

_____

8. $a_1 = 2$ and $a_5 = 162$

9. $a_2 = 30$ and $a_3 = 10$

_____

_____

A bank account earns a constant rate of interest each month. The account was opened on March 1 with $18,000 in it. On April 1, the balance in the account was $18,045. Use this information for 10–12.

10. Write an explicit rule and a recursive rule that can be used to find $A(n)$, the balance after n months.

_____

11. Find the balance after 5 months. _____

12. Find the balance after 5 years. _____

LESSON 15-2 Constructing Geometric Sequences

Practice and Problem Solving: C

Each rule represents a geometric sequence. If the given rule is recursive, write it as an explicit rule. If the rule is explicit, write it as a recursive rule. Assume that $f(1)$ is the first term of the sequence.

1. $f(1) = \dfrac{2}{3}$; $f(n) = f(n-1) \cdot 8$ for $n \geq 2$

2. $f(n) = -10(0.4)^{n-1}$

_____   _____

Write an explicit rule for each geometric sequence based on the given terms from the sequence. Assume that the common ratio r is positive.

3. $a_1 = 6$ and $a_4 = 162$

4. $a_2 = 9$ and $a_4 = 2.25$

_____   _____

5. $a_4 = 0.01$ and $a_5 = 0.0001$

6. $a_3 = \dfrac{1}{48}$ and $a_4 = \dfrac{1}{192}$

_____   _____

7. $a_3 = 32$ and $a_6 = \dfrac{256}{125}$

8. $a_2 = -4$ and $a_4 = -9$

_____   _____

Solve.

9. A geometric sequence contains the terms $a_3 = 40$ and $a_5 = 640$. Write the explicit rules for $r > 0$ and for $r < 0$.

_____

10. The sum of the first n terms of the geometric sequence $f(n) = ar^{n-1}$ can be found using the formula $\dfrac{a(r^n - 1)}{r - 1}$. Use this formula to find the sum $1 + 3 + 3^2 + 3^3 + \dots + 3^{10}$. Check your answer the long way.

_____

11. An account earning interest compounded annually was worth $44,100 after 2 years and $48,620.25 after 4 years. What is the interest rate?

_____

12. There are 64 teams in a basketball tournament. All teams play in the first round but only winning teams move on to subsequent rounds. Write an explicit rule for $T(n)$, the number of games in the nth round of the tournament. State the domain:

_____

Name _____ Date _____ Class_____

Constructing Exponential Functions
Practice and Problem Solving: A/B

Use two points to write an equation for each function shown.

1.

x	0	1	2	3
f(x)	6	18	54	162

_____

2.

x	–2	0	2	4
f(x)	84	21	5.25	1.3125

_____

Complete the table using domain of {–2, –1, 0, 1, 2} for each function shown. Graph each.

3. $f(x) = 3(2)^x$

x	–2	–1	0	1	2
f(x)					

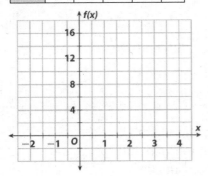

4. $f(x) = 4(0.5)^x$

x	–2	–1	0	1	2
f(x)					

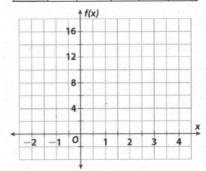

Graph each function.

5. $y = 5(2)^x$

6. $y = -2(3)^x$

7. $y = 3\left(\dfrac{1}{2}\right)^x$

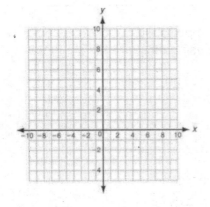
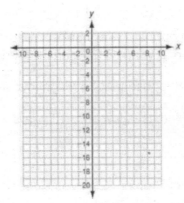
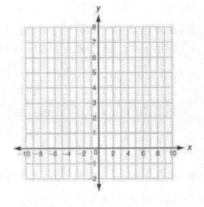

Solve.

8. If a basketball is bounced from a height of 15 feet, the function $f(x) = 15(0.75)^x$ gives the height of the ball in feet at each bounce, where x is the bounce number. What will be the height of the fifth bounce?

Round to the nearest tenth of a foot. _____

Name _____ Date _____ Class_____

Constructing Exponential Functions

Practice and Problem Solving: C

Graph each function. On your graph, include points to indicate the ordered pairs for $x = -1, 0, 1,$ and 2.

1. $f(x) = 0.75(2)^x$

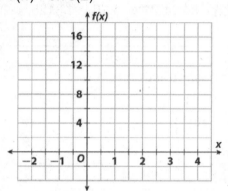

2. $f(x) = 5(4)^{-x}$

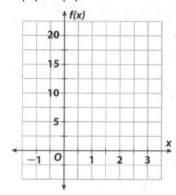

Solve.

3. An exponential function, $f(x)$, passes through the points $(2, 360)$ and $(3, 216)$. Write an equation for $f(x)$.

_____

4. The half-life of a radioactive substance is the average amount of time it takes for half of its atoms to disintegrate. Suppose you started with 200 grams of a substance with a half-life of 3 minutes. How many minutes have passed if 25 grams now remain? Explain your reasoning.

_____

_____

5. If A is deposited in a bank account at $r\%$ annual interest, compounded annually, its value at the end of n years, $V(n)$, can be found using the formula $V(n) = A\left(1 + \dfrac{r}{100}\right)^n$. Suppose that $5000 is invested in an account paying 4% interest. Find its value after 10 years.

_____

6. The graph of $f(x) = 5(4)^{-x}$ from Problem 2 moves closer and closer to the x-axis as x increases. Does the graph ever reach the x-axis? Explain your reasoning and what your conclusion implies about the range of the function.

_____

_____

LESSON 15-4

Graphing Exponential Functions
Practice and Problem Solving: A/B

Graph each exponential function. Identify *a*, *b*, the *y*-intercept, and the end behavior of the graph.

1. $f(x) = 4(2)^x$

x	−2	−1	0	1	2
f(x)					

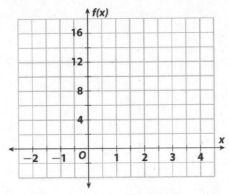

a = _____ *b* = _____ *y*-intercept = _____

end behavior: $x \to -\infty =$ _____ , $x \to +\infty =$ _____

2. $f(x) = \frac{1}{3}(3)^x$

x	−2	−1	0	1	2
f(x)					

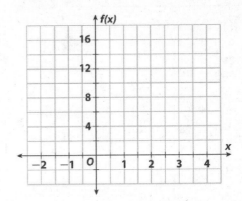

a = _____ *b* = _____ *y*-intercept = _____

end behavior: $x \to -\infty =$ _____ , $x \to +\infty =$ _____

3. $f(x) = -3(2)^x$

x	−2	−1	0	1	2
f(x)					

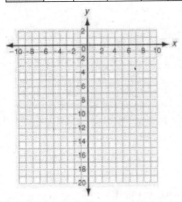

a = _____ *b* = _____ *y*-intercept = _____

end behavior: $x \to -\infty =$ _____ , $x \to +\infty =$ _____

4. $f(x) = 3\left(\frac{1}{2}\right)^x$

x	−2	−1	0	1	2
f(x)					

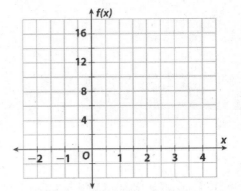

a = _____ *b* = _____ *y*-intercept = _____

end behavior: $x \to -\infty =$ _____ , $x \to +\infty =$ _____

Graphing Exponential Functions
Practice and Problem Solving: C

Graph each exponential function. Identify *a*, *b*, the *y*-intercept, and the end behavior of the graph.

1. $f(x) = 3.5(2)^x$

x	–2	–1	0	1	2
f(x)					

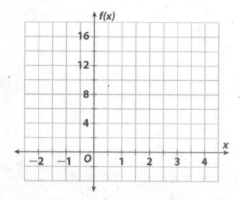

$a =$ ____ $b =$ ____ y-intercept = ____

end behavior: $x \rightarrow -\infty =$ ____ , $x \rightarrow +\infty =$ ____

2. $f(x) = \frac{1}{2}(3)^x$

x	–2	–1	0	1	2
f(x)					

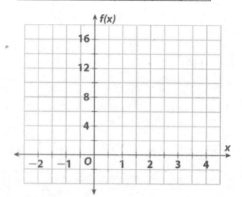

$a =$ ____ $b =$ ____ y-intercept = ____

end behavior: $x \rightarrow -\infty =$ ____ , $x \rightarrow +\infty =$ ____

Graph each function. On your graph, include points to indicate the ordered pairs for *x* = –1, 0, 1, and 2.

3. $f(x) = -3(2)^x$

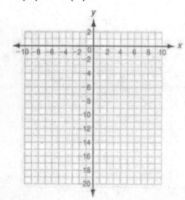

4. $f(x) = 5(4)^{-x}$

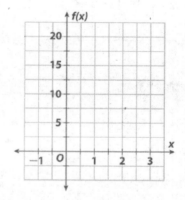

Solve.

5. The half-life of a radioactive substance is the average amount of time it takes for half of its atoms to disintegrate. Suppose you started with 200 grams of a substance with a half-life of 3 minutes. How many minutes have passed if 25 grams now remain? Explain your reasoning.

_____

_____

Transforming Exponential Functions

Practice and Problem Solving: A/B

A parent function has equation $Y_1 = (0.25)^x$. For 1–4, find the equation for each Y_2.

1. Y_2 is a vertical stretch of Y_1. The values of Y_2 are 6 times those of Y_1.

   _____

2. Y_2 is a vertical compression of Y_1. The values of Y_2 are half those of Y_1.

   _____

3. Y_2 is a translation of Y_1 4 units down.

   _____

4. Y_2 is a translation of Y_1 11 units up.

   _____

Values for $f(x)$, a parent function, and $g(x)$, a function in the same family, are shown below. Use the table for 5–8.

x	−2	−1	0	1	2
f(x)	0.04	0.2	1	5	25
g(x)	0.016	0.08	0.4	2	10

5. Write equations for the two functions.

   _____

6. Is $g(x)$ a vertical stretch or a vertical compression of $f(x)$? Explain how you can tell.

   _____

7. Do the graphs of $f(x)$ and $g(x)$ meet at any points? If so, find where. If not, explain why not.

   _____

   _____

8. Let $h(x)$ be the function defined by $h(x) = -f(x)$. Describe how the graph of $h(x)$ is related to the graph of $f(x)$.

   _____

   _____

Name _____ Date _____ Class_____

 # Transforming Exponential Functions
Practice and Problem Solving: C

A parent function has equation $Y_1 = (0.8)^x$. Find the equation
for each Y_2, a function created by transforming Y_1.

1. To form Y_2, there is first a vertical stretch of Y_1 such that the values of
   Y_2 are twice those of Y_1. Then the resulting graph is shifted 8 units up.

   _____

2. To form Y_2, there is first a vertical compression of Y_1 such that the values of Y_2
   are one-third those of Y_1. Then the resulting graph is shifted 12 units down.

   _____

3. To form Y_2, the graph of Y_1 is reflected across the *x*-axis.

   _____

4. To form Y_2, the graph of Y_1 is reflected across the *y*-axis.

   _____

5. To form Y_2, the graph of Y_1 is shifted 3 units down and then reflected
   across the *x*-axis.

   _____

6. To form Y_2, the graph of Y_1 is reflected across the *x*-axis and then
   shifted 3 units up.

   _____

7. To form Y_2, the graph of Y_1 is shifted 10 units down and then reflected
   across the *y*-axis.

   _____

8. To form Y_2, the graph of Y_1 is reflected across the *y*-axis and then
   shifted 10 units down.

   _____

9. To form Y_2, the graph of Y_1 is reflected first across the *x*-axis and then
   across the *y*-axis.

   _____

10. To form Y_2, the graph of Y_1 is reflected across the *x*-axis, then across
    the *y*-axis, then across the *x*-axis again, and finally across the *y*-axis.

    _____

LESSON 16-1

Using Graphs and Properties to Solve Equations with Exponents

Practice and Problem Solving: A/B

Solve each equation without graphing.

1. $5^x = 625$

2. $4(2)^x = 128$

3. $\dfrac{6^x}{16} = 81$

_____   _____   _____

4. $\dfrac{1}{12}(6)^x = 108$

5. $\left(\dfrac{4}{5}\right)^x = \dfrac{64}{125}$

6. $\dfrac{2}{3}\left(\dfrac{1}{2}\right)^x = \dfrac{1}{6}$

_____   _____   _____

7. $\dfrac{2}{5}(10)^x = 40$

8. $(0.1)^x = 0.00001$

9. $\dfrac{2}{3}\left(\dfrac{3}{8}\right)^x = \dfrac{9}{256}$

_____   _____   _____

Solve each equation by graphing. Round your answer to the nearest tenth. Write the equations of the functions you graphed first.

10. $9^x = 11$

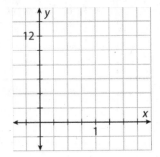

Equation: _____

Equation: _____

Solution: _____

11. $12^x = 120$

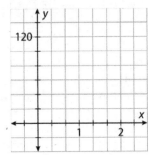

Equation: _____

Equation: _____

Solution: _____

Solve using a graphing calculator. Round your answers to the nearest tenth.

12. A town with a population of 600 is expected to grow at an annual rate of 5%. Write an equation and find the number of years it is expected to take the town to reach a population of 900.

_____

13. How long will it take $20,000 earning 3.5% annual interest to double in value?

_____

Name _____ Date _____ Class_____

Using Graphs and Properties to Solve Equations with Exponents
Practice and Problem Solving: C

Solve each equation without graphing.

1. $\frac{1}{27}(3)^x = 9$

2. $\frac{5}{16}(2)^x = 160$

3. $\frac{25}{27}\left(\frac{3}{5}\right)^x = \frac{3}{25}$

_____ _____ _____

4. $\frac{1}{2}\left(\frac{1}{2}\right)^x = \frac{1}{2}$

5. $\left(\frac{7}{11}\right)^x = \frac{11}{7}$

6. $\left(\frac{1}{8}\right)^x = 64$

_____ _____ _____

Solve each equation by graphing. Round your answer to the nearest tenth.

7. $(2.72)^x = 3.14$

8. $16(3)^x = 40$

9. $\frac{1}{7}\left(\frac{7}{8}\right)^x = \frac{3}{50}$

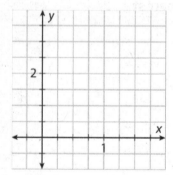 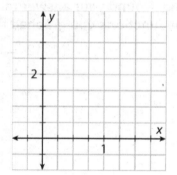 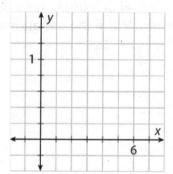

_____ _____ _____

Solve using a graphing calculator.

10. Does $10,000 invested at 6% interest double its value in half the time as $10,000 invested at 3% interest? Show your work.

_____

_____

11. Suppose you were a Revolutionary War veteran and had the foresight to put one penny in a bank account when George Washington became President in 1789. If the bank promised you 5% interest on your account, how much would it be worth in 2014?

_____

_____

LESSON 16-2

Modeling Exponential Growth and Decay

Practice and Problem Solving: A/B

Write an exponential growth function to model each situation. Determine the domain and range of each function. Then find the value of the function after the given amount of time.

1. Annual sales for a fast food restaurant are $650,000 and are increasing at a rate of 4% per year; 5 years

   _____

   _____

2. The population of a school is 800 students and is increasing at a rate of 2% per year; 6 years

   _____

   _____

Write an exponential decay function to model each situation. Determine the domain and range of each function. Then find the value of the function after the given amount of time.

3. The population of a town is 2500 and is decreasing at a rate of 3% per year; 5 years

   _____

   _____

4. The value of a company's equipment is $25,000 and decreases at a rate of 15% per year; 8 years

   _____

   _____

Write an exponential growth or decay function to model each situation. Then graph each function.

5. The population is 20,000 now and expected to grow at an annual rate of 5%.

   _____

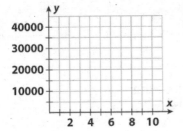

6. A boat that cost $45,000 is depreciating at a rate of 20% per year.

   _____

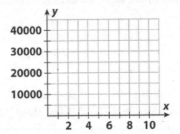

Name _____ Date _____ Class _____

Modeling Exponential Growth and Decay
Practice and Problem Solving: C

Use this information for Problems 1–4.

Odette has two investments that she purchased at the same time.
Investment 1 cost $10,000 and earns 4% interest each year.
Investment 2 cost $8000 and earns 6% interest each year.

1. Write exponential growth functions that could be used to find $v_1(t)$ and $v_2(t)$, the values of the investments after t years.

   _____

2. Find the value of each investment after 5 years. Explain why the difference between their values, which was initially $2000, is now significantly less.

   _____

   _____

3. Will the value of Investment 2 ever exceed the value of Investment 1? If not, why not? If so, when?

   _____

   _____

4. Instead of calculating 4% interest for one year, suppose the interest for Investment 1 was calculated every day at a rate of (4/365)%. This is called daily compounding. Would Odette earn more, the same, or less using this daily method for one year? Provide an example to show your thinking.

   _____

   _____

Solve.

5. A car depreciates in value by 20% each year. Graham argued that the value of the car after 5 years must be $0, since 20% × 5 = 100%. Do you agree or disagree? Explain fully.

   _____

   _____

6. Workers at a plant suffered pay cuts of 10% during a recession. When the economy returned to normal, their salaries were raised 10%. Should the workers be satisfied? Explain your thinking.

   _____

   _____

Name _____ Date _____ Class_____

Using Exponential Regression Models

LESSON 16-3

Practice and Problem Solving: A/B

The table below shows the total attendance at major league baseball
games, at 10-year intervals since 1930. Use the table for the problems
that follow.

Major League Baseball Total Attendance (y_d), in millions, vs. Years Since 1930 (x)									
x	0	10	20	30	40	50	60	70	80
y_d	10.1	9.8	17.5	19.9	28.7	43.0	54.8	72.6	73.1
y_m									
residual									

1. Use a graphing calculator to find the exponential regression equation
   for this data. Round *a* and *b* to the nearest thousandth.

   _____

2. According to the regression equation, by what percent is attendance
   growing each year?

   _____

3. Complete the row labeled y_m above. This row contains the predicted
   y-values for each *x*-value. Round your answers to the nearest tenth.

4. Calculate the row of residuals above.

5. Analyze the residuals from your table. Does it seem like the equation is
   a good fit for the data?

   _____

   _____

6. Use your graphing calculator to find the correlation coefficient for the
   equation and write it below. Does the correlation coefficient make it
   seem like the equation is a good fit for the data?

   _____

7. Use the exponential regression equation to predict major league
   baseball attendance in 2020. Based on your earlier work on this page,
   do you think this is a reasonable prediction? Explain.

   _____

   _____

Name _____ Date _____ Class_____

LESSON
16-3

Using Exponential Regression Models
Practice and Problem Solving: C

A pot of boiling water is allowed to cool for 50 minutes. The table below shows the temperature of the water as it cools. Use the table for the problems that follow.

Temperature of Water (y_d), in degrees Celsius, after cooling for x minutes											
x	0	5	10	15	20	25	30	35	40	45	50
y_d	100	75	57	44	34	26	21	17	14	11	10
y_m											
residual											

1. Use a graphing calculator to find the exponential regression equation for this data. Round a and b to the nearest thousandth.

_____

2. Complete the rows labeled y_m (predicted y-values) and residual above. Round your answers to the nearest tenth.

3. Fit a linear regression equation to the original data. Write the equation here.

_____

4. The data for the scatter plot is shown in the first two rows of the table below. Complete the next two rows of the table for the model you found in Problem 3.

Temperature of Water (y_d), in degrees Celsius, after cooling for x minutes											
x	0	5	10	15	20	25	30	35	40	45	50
y_d	100	75	57	44	34	26	21	17	14	11	10
y_m											
residual											

5. Examine the residuals in each table. Which appears to be the better model—the linear or exponential equation? Explain.

_____

_____

6. Find the correlation coefficients for the two equations. Based on that information, which equation is the better model? Explain.

_____

Comparing Linear and Exponential Models

LESSON
16-4

Practice and Problem Solving: A/B

Without graphing, tell whether each quantity is changing at a constant amount per unit interval, at a constant percent per unit interval, or neither. Justify your reasoning.

1. A bank account started with $1000 and earned $10 interest per month for two years. The bank then paid 2% interest on the account for the next two years.

   _____

2. Jin Lu earns a bonus for each sale she makes. She earns $100 for the first sale, $150 for the second sale, $200 for the third sale, and so on.

   _____

Use this information for Problems 3–8.

A bank offers annual rates of 6% simple interest or 5% compound interest on its savings accounts. Suppose you have $10,000 to invest.

3. Express $f(x)$, the value of your deposit after x years in the simple interest account, and $g(x)$, the value of your deposit after x years in the compound interest account.

   _____

4. Is either $f(x)$ or $g(x)$ a linear function? An exponential function? How can you tell?

   _____

5. Find the values of your deposit after three years in each account. After three years, which account is the better choice?

   _____

6. Find the values of your deposit after 20 years in each account. After 20 years, which account is the better choice?

   _____

7. Use a graphing calculator to determine the length of time an account must be held for the two choices to be equally attractive. Round your answer to the nearest tenth.

   _____

8. Use your answer to Problem 7 to write a statement that advises an investor regarding how to choose between the two accounts.

   _____

Comparing Linear and Exponential Models

LESSON 16-4

Practice and Problem Solving: C

Without graphing, tell whether each quantity is changing at a constant amount per unit interval, at a constant percent per unit interval, or neither. Justify your reasoning.

1. When Josh read his first book alone, his mother gave him a penny. For his second book, she gave him two cents, and for his third book, she gave him four cents. She plans on doubling the amount for each book Josh reads.

   _____

2. The annual cost of a club membership starts at $100 and increases by $15 each year.

   _____

Use this information for Problems 3–7.

A bank offers annual rates of 4% simple interest or 3.5% compound interest on its savings accounts.

3. Express the values of an initial investment of A dollars after x years. Let $f(x)$ represent the amount in a simple interest account and let $g(x)$ represent the amount in a compound interest account.

   _____

4. If you planned on depositing money for three years, which rate would be a better choice? Explain.

   _____

   _____

5. If you planned on depositing money for 15 years, which rate would be a better choice? Explain.

   _____

   _____

6. Determine the length of time an account must be held for the two choices to be equally attractive. (HINT: You may want to graph the equations.) Round to the nearest tenth.

   _____

7. Would the amount deposited affect any of the answers you gave for Problems 4–6? Justify your reasoning.

   _____

LESSON 17-1 **Understanding Polynomial Expressions**

Practice and Problem Solving: A/B

Identify each expression as a monomial, a binomial, a trinomial, or none of the above. Write the degree of each expression.

1. $6b^2 - 7$

   _____

2. $x^2y - 9x^4y^2 + 3xy$

   _____

3. $35r^3s$

   _____

4. $3p + \dfrac{2p}{q} - 5q$

   _____

5. $4ab^5 + 2ab - 3a^4b^3$

   _____

6. $st + t^{0.5}$

   _____

Simplify each expression.

7. $6n^3 - n^2 + 3n^4 + 5n^2$

   _____

8. $c^3 + c^2 + 2c - 3c^3 - c^2 - 4c$

   _____

9. $11b^2 + 3b - 1 - 2b^2 - 2b - 8$

   _____

10. $a^4b^3 + 9a^3b^4 - 3a^4b^3 - 4a^3b^4$

    _____

11. $9xy + 5x^2 + 15x - 10xy$

    _____

12. $3p^2q + 8p^3 - 2p^2q + 2p + 5p^3$

    _____

Determine the polynomial that has the greater value for the given value of x.

13. $4x^2 - 5x - 2$ or $5x^2 - 2x - 4$ for $x = 6$

    _____

14. $6x^3 - 4x^2 + 7$ or $7x^3 - 6x^2 + 4$ for $x = 3$

    _____

Solve.

15. A rocket is launched from the top of an 80-foot cliff with an initial velocity of 88 feet per second. The height of the rocket t seconds after launch is given by the equation $h = -16t^2 + 88t + 80$. How high will the rocket be after 2 seconds?

    _____

16. Antoine is making a banner in the shape of a triangle. He wants to line the banner with a decorative border. How long will the border be?

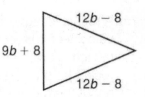

$12b - 8$

$9b + 8$

$12b - 8$

    _____

LESSON
17-1

Understanding Polynomial Expressions
Practice and Problem Solving: C

Simplify each expression. Then identify the expression as a monomial, a binomial, a trinomial, or none of the above. Write the degree of each polynomial.

1. $6ab^2 - 3a^2b - 3ab^2$

2. $5xy - 9x + 3xy + 2y^2$

_____

3. $-\sqrt{16y^3}$

4. $3n^2 + 9n - 6 + 2n + 6$

_____

5. $4b^5 + 2b^2 - 3b^6 - 7b^5 - b^2 + 3b^5$

6. $\sqrt{\dfrac{9x}{25}}$

_____

Simplify each expression.

7. $6mn^3 - mn^2 + 3mn^3 + 15mn^2$

8. $1.6c^3 + 5.6c^2 + 2.5c - 3.7c^3 + 7.3c^2 - 4.9c$

_____

9. $11\dfrac{2}{3}b^2 + 3\dfrac{1}{4}b - 6\dfrac{5}{6} - 2\dfrac{1}{2}b^2 + 4\dfrac{1}{3}b + 1\dfrac{11}{12}$

10. $a^4b^3 + 8a^3b^4 - 2a^2b^5 - 6a^4b^3 - 9a^3b^4$

_____

11. $5.2x^2 + 5.1x - 7.3xy + 6.4x^2 - 2.4x + 1.8xy$

12. $8\dfrac{1}{2}p^3 + \dfrac{7}{8}pq + 5\dfrac{3}{4}p^3 - 2\dfrac{1}{3}pq$

_____

Determine the polynomial that has the greater value for the given value of *x*. Then, determine how much greater it is than the other polynomial.

13. $4x^2 - 5x - 2$ or $5x^2 - 2x - 4$ for $x = 1.5$

14. $6x^3 - 4x^2 + 7$ or $7x^3 - 6x^2 + 4$ for $x = -3$

_____

Solve.

15. A rocket is launched from the top of an 80-foot cliff with an initial velocity of 88 feet per second. The height of the rocket *t* seconds after launch is given by the equation $h = -16t^2 + 88t + 80$. How high will the rocket be after 2 seconds? After 3.5 seconds? What do you notice about the heights? Explain your answer.

_____

_____

LESSON 17-2 Adding Polynomial Expressions
Practice and Problem Solving: A/B

Add the polynomial expressions using the vertical format.

1.
$$(10g^2 + 3g - 10)$$
$$+ (2g^2 + g + 9)$$
_____

2.
$$(4x^3 + x^2 + 2x)$$
$$+ (3x^3 + x^2 + 4x)$$
_____

3.
$$(11b^2 + 3b - 1)$$
$$+ (2b^2 + 2b + 8)$$
_____

4.
$$(c^3 + 2c^2 + 2c)$$
$$+ (-3c^3 + c^2 - 4c)$$
_____

5.
$$(ab^2 + 13b - 4a)$$
$$+ (3ab^2 + a + 7b)$$
_____

6.
$$(-r^2 + 8pr - p)$$
$$+ (-12r^2 - 2pr + 8p)$$
_____

Add the polynomial expressions using the horizontal format.

7. $(3y^2 - y + 3) + (2y^2 + 2y + 9)$

8. $(4z^3 + 3z^2 + 8) + (2z^3 + z^2 - 3)$

9. $(6s^3 + 9s + 10) + (3s^3 + 4s - 10)$

10. $(15a^4 + 6a^2 + a) + (6a^4 - 2a^2 + a)$

11. $(-7a^2b^3 + 3a^3b - 9ab) + (4a^2b^3 - 5a^3b + ab)$ 12. $(2p^4q^2 + 5p^3q - 2pq) + (8p^4q^2 - 3p^3q - pq)$

Solve.

13. A rectangular picture frame has the dimensions shown in the figure. Write a polynomial that represents the perimeter of the frame.

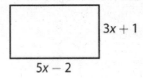

$3x + 1$

$5x - 2$

_____

Adding Polynomial Expressions

Practice and Problem Solving: C

Simplify.

1. $(ab^2 + 13b - 9) + (6 - 4a + 3ab^2) + (a + 7b)$

   _____

2. $(9x^3 - 2x^2 - x) + (3x + x^3 - 4) + (x^2 - 3x)$

   _____

3. $(-r^2 + 8pr - p) + (-12r^2 - 2pr) + (8p + 3r^2)$

   _____

4. $(rs^2 - s - 6) + (2rs^2 - 3s + 1) + (s + 4rs^2)$

   _____

5. What algebraic expression must be added to the sum of
   $3x^2 + 4x + 8$ and $2x^2 - 6x + 3$ to give $9x^2 - 2x - 5$ as the result?

   _____

Give an example for each statement.

6. The sum of two binomials is a monomial.

   _____

7. The sum of two trinomials is a binomial.

   _____

Solve.

8. The sum of the squares of the first n positive integers is $\dfrac{n^3}{3} + \dfrac{n^2}{2} + \dfrac{n}{6}$.

   The sum of the cubes of the first n positive integers is $\dfrac{n^4}{4} + \dfrac{n^3}{2} + \dfrac{n^2}{4}$.

   Write an expression for the sum of the squares and cubes of the first n
   positive integers. Then find the sum of the first 10 squares and cubes.

   _____

9. Vincent is going to frame the rectangular picture with
   dimensions shown. The frame will be $x + 1$ inches wide.
   Find the perimeter of the frame.

   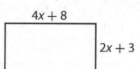

   _____

LESSON 17-3

Subtracting Polynomial Expressions

Practice and Problem Solving: A/B

Subtract using the vertical form.

1. $(5g^2 + 6g - 10)$
   $- (2g^2 + 2g + 9)$
   _____

2. $(8x^3 + 4x^2 + x)$
   $- (2x^3 + x^2 + x)$
   _____

3. $(10b^2 + 5b - 2)$
   $- (2b^2 + b + 1)$
   _____

4. $(7c^3 - 5c^2 + 2c)$
   $- (-3c^3 + 2c^2 - 2c)$
   _____

5. $(14ab^2 + 9b - 2a)$
   $- (4ab^2 + 2a + 5b)$
   _____

6. $(6x^3 + 2x^2 + 3x)$
   $- (3x^3 - 2x^2 - 3x)$
   _____

Subtract using the horizontal form.

7. $(7y^2 - 7y + 7) - (4y^2 + 2y + 3)$

8. $(11z^3 + 6z^2 + 3) - (9z^3 + 2z^2 - 8)$

9. $(9s^3 + 10s + 8) - (2s^3 + 9s - 11)$

10. $(25a^4 + 9a^2 + 3a) - (24a^4 - 5a^2 + 3a)$

11. $(-a^2b^3 + a^3b - ab) - (a^2b^3 - a^3b + ab)$

12. $(3p^4q^2 + 8p^3q - 2) - (5p^4q^2 - 2p^3q - 8)$

Solve.

13. Darnell and Stephanie have competing refreshment stand businesses.
    Darnell's profit can be modeled with the polynomial $c^2 + 8c - 100$,
    where c is the number of items sold. Stephanie's profit can be modeled
    with the polynomial $2c^2 - 7c - 200$. Write a polynomial that represents
    the difference between Stephanie's profit and Darnell's profit.

14. There are two boxes in a storage unit. The volume of the first box is
    $4x^3 + 4x^2$ cubic units. The volume of the second box is $6x^3 - 18x^2$
    cubic units. Write a polynomial to show the difference between the two
    volumes.

LESSON
17-3 # Subtracting Polynomial Expressions

Practice and Problem Solving: C

Simplify.

1. $(ab^2 + 13b - 9) - (6 - 4a + 3ab^2) + (a + 7b)$ 2. $(9x^3 - 2x^2 - x) + (3x + x^3 - 4) - (x^2 - 3x)$

_____   _____

3. $(-r^2 + 8pr - p) - (-12r^2 - 2pr) + (8p + 3r^2)$ 4. $(rs^2 - s - 6) + (2rs^2 - 3s + 1) - (s + 4rs^2)$

_____   _____

5. What algebraic expression must be subtracted from the sum of
   $y^2 + 5y - 1$ and $3y^2 - 2y + 4$ to give $2y^2 + 7y - 2$ as the result?

   _____

Give an example for each statement.

6. The difference of two binomials is a binomial.   7. The difference of two binomials is a
                                                         trinomial.

   _____   _____

Solve.

8. Ned, Tony, Matt, and Juan are playing basketball. Ned scored $2p + 3$
   points, Tony scored 3 more points than Ned, Matt scored twice as
   many points as Tony, and Juan scored 8 fewer points than Ned. Write
   an expression that represents the total number of points scored by all
   four boys.

   _____

9. Mr. Watford owns two car dealerships. His profit from the first can be
   modeled with the polynomial $c^3 - c^2 + 2c - 100$, where c is the number
   of cars he sells. Mr. Watford's profit from his second dealership can be
   modeled with the polynomial $c^2 - 4c - 300$.

   a. Write a polynomial to represent the difference of the profit at his first
      dealership and the profit at his second dealership.

      _____

   b. If Mr. Watford sells 45 cars in his first dealership and 300 cars in
      his second, what is the difference in profit between the two dealerships?

      _____

LESSON 18-1 Multiplying Polynomial Expressions by Monomials

Practice and Problem Solving: A/B

Find the product.

1. $5x(2x^4y^3)$

   _____

2. $0.5p(-30p^3r^2)$

   _____

3. $11ab^2(2a^5b^4)$

   _____

4. $-6c^3d^5(-3c^2d)$

   _____

5. $4(3a^2 + 2a - 7)$

   _____

6. $9x^2(x^3 - 4x^2 - 3x)$

   _____

7. $6s^3(-2s^2 + 4s - 10)$

   _____

8. $5a^4(6a^4 - 2a^2 - a)$

   _____

9. $8pr(-7r^2 - 2pr + 8p)$

   _____

10. $2mn^3(3mn^3 + n^2 + 4mn)$

    _____

11. $-3x^4y^2(2x^2 + 5xy + 9y^2)$

    _____

12. $0.75\ v^2w^3(12v^3 + 16v^2w - 8w^2)$

    _____

13. $-7a^2b^3(4a^2b^3 + ab - 5a^3b)$

    _____

14. $2p^4q^2(8p^4q^2 - 3p^3q + 5p^2q)$

    _____

Solve.

15. The length of a rectangle is 3 inches greater than the width.

    a. Write a polynomial expression that represents

       the area of the rectangle.   _____

    b. Find the area of the rectangle when the

       width is 4 inches.   _____

16. The length of a rectangle is 8 centimeters less than 3 times the width.

    a. Write a polynomial expression that represents

       the area of the rectangle.   _____

    b. Find the area of the rectangle when the

       width is 10 centimeters.   _____

LESSON
18-1
Multiplying Polynomial Expressions by Monomials

Practice and Problem Solving: C

Find the product.

1. $\frac{1}{3}m^3(6m)(2m^2)$

_____

2. $-3x^4(12x)(0.75x^4)$

_____

3. $\frac{2}{3}xy^2(xy)\left(\frac{1}{2}x\right)$

_____

4. $-6c^3d^5(-3c^2d)(-2cd)$

_____

5. $\frac{1}{2}x(6x^2 + 10x + 5)$

_____

6. $0.4x(5x^3 - 8x^2 - 1.4x)$

_____

Simplify.

7. $\frac{3}{4}v^2(4v^3 + 16v^2 - 8v) - 3v(v^4 + 4v^3 - 2)$

_____

8. $5a^4(6a^4 - 2a^2 - a) - 2a(a^7 + 5a^5 - 3)$

_____

9. $6s^3(-2s^2 + 4s - 10) + 3s(4s^4 - 8s^3 + 5s^2)$

_____

10. $2jk^3(3jk^3 + j^2 + 4jk) - jk(9j^2k^2 + jk^3)$

_____

11. $-3x^4y^2(2x^2 + 5xy + 9y^2) - xy(2x^3y^3 - x^4y^2)$

_____

12. $8pr(7r^2 - 2pr + p) + 3r(-5pr^2 + 6p^2r - 8p^2)$

_____

Solve.

13. The shaded area represents the deck around a swimming pool. Write a polynomial expression in simplest form for the following.

   a. the area of the swimming pool

   _____

   b. the total area of the swimming pool and deck

   _____

   c. the area of the deck _____

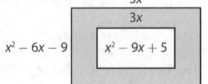

14. Write four multiplication problems that have a product of $24a^3b^2 - 16a^2b$.

_____

LESSON 18-2

Multiplying Polynomial Expressions

Practice and Problem Solving: A/B

Multiply.

1. $(x + 5)(x + 6)$

   _____

2. $(a - 7)(a - 3)$

   _____

3. $(d + 8)(d - 4)$

   _____

4. $(2x - 3)(x + 4)$

   _____

5. $(5b + 1)(b - 2)$

   _____

6. $(3p - 2)(2p + 3)$

   _____

7. $(5k - 9)(2k - 4)$

   _____

8. $(2m - 5)(3m + 8)$

   _____

9. $(4 + 7g)(5 - 8g)$

   _____

10. $(r + 2s)(r - 6s)$

    _____

11. $(3 - 2v)(2 - 5v)$

    _____

12. $(5 + h)(5 - h)$

    _____

13. $(y + 3)(y - 3)$

    _____

14. $(z - 5)^2$

    _____

15. $(3q + 7)(3q - 7)$

    _____

16. $(4w + 9)^2$

    _____

17. $(3a - 4)^2$

    _____

18. $(5q - 8r)(5q + 8r)$

    _____

19. $(x + 4)(x^2 + 3x + 5)$

    _____

20. $(3m + 4)(m^2 - 3m + 5)$

    _____

21. $(2x - 5)(4x^2 - 3x + 1)$

    _____

Solve.

22. Write a polynomial expression that represents the area of the trapezoid. $\left(A = \frac{1}{2}h(b_1 + b_2) \right)$

    _____

23. If $x = 4$ in., find the area of the trapezoid in problem 22.

    _____

24. Kayla worked $3x + 6$ hours this week. She earns $x - 2$ dollars per hour. Write a polynomial expression that represents the amount Kayla earned this week. Then calculate her pay for the week if $x = 11$.

    _____

LESSON
18-2
Multiplying Polynomial Expressions
Practice and Problem Solving: C

Multiply.

1. $2(x + 5)(x + 6)$

2. $3(a - 7)(a - 3)$

3. $-5(8 + d)(4 - d)$

_____ _____ _____

4. $4(2x - 3)(x + 4)$

5. $6(5b + 1)(b - 2)$

6. $-2(3p - 2)(2p + 3)$

_____ _____ _____

7. $2k(5k - 9)(2k - 4)$

8. $m^2(2m - 5)(3m + 8)$

9. $-8g^2(4 + 7g)(5 - 8g)$

_____ _____ _____

10. $rs(r + 2s)(r - 6s)$

11. $4v(3 - 2v)(2 - 5v)$

12. $6h^2(5 + 9h)(5 - 9h)$

_____ _____ _____

13. $y(2y^2 + 3)(2y^2 - 3)$

14. $3(6z - 5)^2$

15. $4c(3c + 7d)(3c - 7d)$

_____ _____ _____

16. $-3w(4w + 9)^2$

17. $2a(3a - 4)^2$

18. $qr(5q^2 - 8r^2)(5q^2 + 8r^2)$

_____ _____ _____

19. $(3x - 1)(2x^2 - 3x - 7)$

20. $(5z + 6)(2z + 1)(2z - 1)$

21. $(x + 2)(5x - 3)^2$

_____ _____ _____

Solve.

22. Write a polynomial expression that represents the volume of the cube.

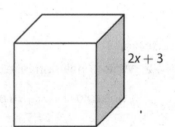
$2x + 3$

_____

23. Explain how you can use the polynomial expression to find the volume of the cube in problem 22 if $x = 4$ in. Then find the volume when $x = 4$ in. How can you check your answer?

_____

_____

24. Multiply $(n - 1)(n + 1)$, $(n - 1)(n^2 + n + 1)$, and $(n - 1)(n^3 + n^2 + n + 1)$. Describe the pattern of the products. Use the pattern to find $(n - 1)(n^4 + n^3 + n^2 + n + 1)$.

_____

_____

Special Products of Binomials
Practice and Problem Solving: A/B

Find the product.

1. $(x+2)^2$

    _____

2. $(m+4)^2$

    _____

3. $(3+a)^2$

    _____

4. $(2x+5)^2$

    _____

5. $(8-y)^2$

    _____

6. $(a-10)^2$

    _____

7. $(b-3)^2$

    _____

8. $(3x-7)^2$

    _____

9. $(6-3n)^2$

    _____

10. $(x+3)(x-3)$

    _____

11. $(8+y)(8-y)$

    _____

12. $(x+6)(x-6)$

    _____

13. $(5x+2)(5x-2)$

    _____

14. $(4+2y)(4-2y)$

    _____

15. $(10x+7y)(10x-7y)$

    _____

Solve.

16. Write a simplified expression for each of the following.

    a. area of the large rectangle

        _____

    b. area of the small rectangle

        _____

    c. area of the shaded area

        _____

17. The small rectangle is made larger by adding 2 units to the length and 2 units to the width.

    a. What is the new area of the smaller rectangle?

        _____

    b. What is the area of the new shaded area?

        _____

Name _____ Date _____ Class_____

Special Products of Binomials

Practice and Problem Solving: C

Find the product.

1. $(3x + 1)^2$

2. $(5m + 0.5)^2$

3. $(7 + 2a)^2$

_____   _____   _____

4. $(2x + 3y)^2$

5. $(2a^2 + 9b)^2$

6. $(5a^2 + 4b^2)^2$

_____   _____   _____

7. $\left(\dfrac{1}{4} - y^2\right)^2$

8. $\left(\dfrac{1}{2} + y\right)\left(\dfrac{1}{2} - y\right)$

9. $\left(\dfrac{1}{2}a^3 - 3\right)^2$

_____   _____   _____

10. $(x + 0.6)(x - 0.6)$

11. $(3x^3 - 7)^2$

12. $(x + 0.25)(x - 0.25)$

_____   _____   _____

13. $(a^2b + ab)(a^2b - ab)$

14. $(0.8x^2 + y^2)(0.8x^2 - y^2)$

15. $(4x^3y + 5x)(4x^3y - 5x)$

_____   _____   _____

Solve.

16. Write a simplified expression for each of the following.

    a. area of the large rectangle

    _____

    b. area of the small rectangle

    _____

    c. area of the shaded area

    _____

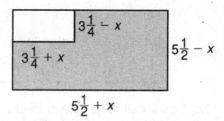

17. A rectangle has a length $(x + 3.5)$ and an area of $x^2 - 12.25$. What is the width of the rectangle?

_____

Name _____ Date _____ Class_____

Understanding Quadratic Functions
Practice and Problem Solving: A/B

For Exercises 1–4, tell whether the graph of the function

  a. opens upward or downward

  b. has a maximum or minimum

  c. is a reflection across the *x*-axis of the parent function

  d. is a stretch or a compression (shrink)?

1. $y = 4x^2$

_____

_____

2. $y = -5x^2$

_____

_____

3. $y = -3.2x^2$

_____

_____

4. $y = 0.4x^2$

_____

_____

Determine the characteristics of each quadratic function.

5. $y = 1.5x^2$

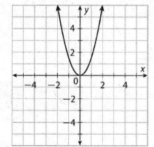

6. $y = -2.5x^2$

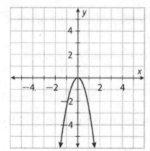

Vertex: _____

Minimum (if any): _____

Maximum (if any): _____

Parent function reflected across

x-axis? _____

Stretch or shrink? _____

Vertex: _____

Minimum (if any): _____

Maximum (if any): _____

Parent function reflected across

x-axis? _____

Stretch or shrink? _____

Solve.

7. A quadratic function has the form $y = ax^2$ for some nonzero value of *a*
   and (4, 48) is on the graph. What is the value of *a*? _____

LESSON	**Understanding Quadratic Functions**
19-1	

Practice and Problem Solving: C

Solve.

1. The graph of a quadratic function contains (4, –64) and its vertex is at the origin.

    a. Write an equation for this function.

    _____

    b. Does the equation show a stretch or a shrink of its parent equation?

    _____

2. The diagram shows the graph of a quadratic function *f*. Point *P* is on the graph.

    a. Write an equation for this function.

    _____

    b. Does the equation show a stretch or a shrink of its parent equation?

    _____

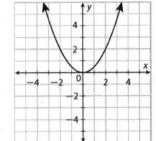

3. The axis of symmetry of the graph of a quadratic function is $x = 0$.
   The vertex has coordinates (0, 0).
   Point (–2, –10) is on the graph.
   Write an equation for the function. _____

4. The table represents three points on the graph of a quadratic function.

    Write an equation for the function. _____

x	y
–3	–31.5
0	0
3	–31.5

5. A quadratic function has the form $y = ax^2$ for some nonzero value of *a*. Suppose that (m, n) is on the graph of the function for some nonzero real numbers *m* and *n*. Show that $a = \dfrac{n}{m^2}$.

    _____

    _____

    _____

6. Functions *f* and *g* have the form $y = ax^2$. The graph of *f* contains (1, 5). The graph of *g* contains (1, 0.2). Which function has a graph wider than that of $y = x^2$? Explain.

    _____

    _____

LESSON
19-2

Transforming Quadratic Functions

Practice and Problem Solving: A/B

A parabola has the equation $f(x) = 2(x - 3)^2 - 4$. Complete:

1. The vertex is _____. 　　2. The graph opens _____.

3. The function has a minimum value of _____.

The following graph is a translation of $y = x^2$. Use it for 4–6.

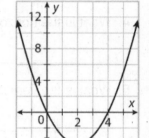

4. What is the horizontal translation?

_____

5. What is the vertical translation?

_____

6. What is the quadratic equation for the graph? _____

Graph the following parabolas.

7. $y = -2(x + 1)^2 + 2$

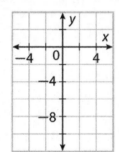

8. $y = \dfrac{1}{2}(x - 2)^2 - 3$

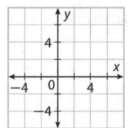

A ball follows a parabolic path represented by $f(x) = -2(x - 5)^2 + 9$.
Use this equation for 9–12.

9. What is the vertex? _____

10. What is the axis of symmetry? _____

11. Find two points on either side of the axis.

_____ and _____

12. Graph the parabola.

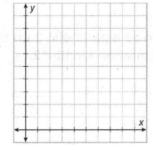

Name _____ Date _____ Class_____

Transforming Quadratic Functions
Practice and Problem Solving: C

A parabola has the equation $f(x) = -2(x - 3)^2 + 4$. Complete:

1. The vertex is _____.

2. The graph opens _____.

3. The function has a minimum value of _____.

The following graph is a translation of $y = x^2$. Use it for 4–7.

4. What is the horizontal translation?

   _____

5. What is the vertical translation?

   _____

6. What is the sign of a?

   _____

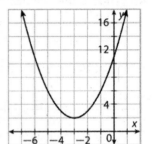

7. What is the quadratic equation for the graph? _____

Graph the following parabolas.

8. $y = -2(x + 2)^2 + 5$

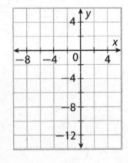

9. $y = \frac{1}{2}(x - 3)^2 - 2$

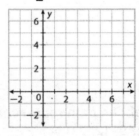

A ball follows a parabolic path represented by $f(x) = -2(x - 4)^2 + 8$.
Use this equation for 10–12.

10. What is the vertex? _____

11. Graph the parabola.

12. Why does the graph stop at $x = 2$ and $x = 6$?

   _____

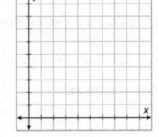

LESSON 19-3 Interpreting Vertex Form and Standard Form

Practice and Problem Solving: A/B

Determine if each function is a quadratic function.

1. $y = 2x^2 - 3x + 5$ 2. $y = 2x - 4$ 3. $y = 2^x + 3x - 4$

_____   _____   _____

Write each quadratic function in standard form and write the equation for the line of symmetry.

4. $y = x + 2 + x^2$ 5. $y = -1 + 2x - x^2$ 6. $y = 2x - 5x^2 - 2$

_____   _____   _____

Change the vertex form to standard quadratic form.

7. $y = 2(x + 3)^2 - 6$ 8. $y = 3(x - 5)^2 + 4$

_____   _____

Use the values in the table to write a quadratic equation in vertex form, then write the function in standard form.

9. The vertex of the function is (1, –3).   10. The vertex of the function is (–3, –2).

x	y
–1	17
0	2
1	–3
2	2
3	17

x	y
–1	14
–2	2
–3	–2
–4	2
–5	14

_____   _____

_____   _____

11. The graph of a function in the form $f(x) = a(x - h)^2 + k$ is shown. Use the graph to find an equation for $f(x)$.

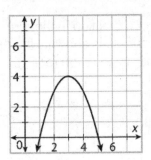

_____

Name _____ Date _____ Class_____

Interpreting Vertex Form and Standard Form
Practice and Problem Solving: C

Determine if each function is a quadratic function.

1. $y = 0.5x^2 - 3$

2. $y = 2(x-4)^2 - 5$

3. $y = 2^x + 3x + 24$

_____ _____ _____

Write each quadratic function in standard form and write the equation for the line of symmetry.

4. $y = 3x + 2 + 2x^2$

5. $y = -0.5 + 1.5x - 2x^2$

6. $y = -2 - 5x^2$

_____ _____ _____

Change the vertex form to standard quadratic form.

7. $y = 3(x + 0.5)^2 - 2.4$

8. $y = -\dfrac{3}{2}(2x - 5)^2 + \dfrac{7}{2}$

_____ _____

Use the values in the table to write a quadratic equation in vertex form, then write the function in standard form.

9. The vertex of the function is (1, 2).

x	y
−1	8
0	3.5
1	2
2	3.5
3	8

10. The vertex of the function is (3, 5).

x	y
1	−23
2	−2
3	5
4	−2
5	−23

_____ _____

_____ _____

11. The graph of a function in the form $f(x) = a(x - h)^2 + k$ is shown. Use the graph to find an equation for $f(x)$.

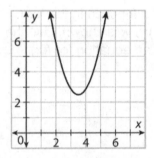

_____

LESSON
20-1
Connecting Intercepts and Zeros
Practice and Problem Solving: A/B

Solve each equation by writing the related function, creating a table of values, graphing the related function, and finding its zeroes.

1. $x^2 + 1 = 2x$

y = _____

x	−1	0	1	2	3
y					

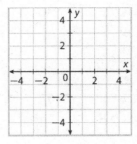

_____

2. $-2x^2 - 2x = 2x$

y = _____

x	−3	−2	−1	0	1
y					

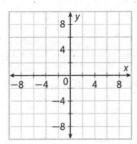

_____

Create a quadratic equation then solve the equation with a related function. You can use a table, graph, or graphing calculator.

3. A skydiver jumps out of a plane 5,000 feet above the ground and her parachute opens 3,000 feet above the ground. The function $h(t) = -16t^2 + 5,000$, where t represents the time in seconds, gives the height h, in feet, of the skydiver as she falls. When does her parachute open? Round to the nearest second.

_____

4. An astronaut on the moon drops a tool from the door of the landing ship. The quadratic function $f(x) = -2x^2 + 10$ models the height of the tool, in meters, after x seconds. How long does it take the tool to hit the surface of the moon? Round your answer to the nearest tenth.

_____

LESSON
20-1

Connecting Intercepts and Zeros

Practice and Problem Solving: C

Solve each equation by writing the related function, creating a table of values, graphing the related function, and finding its zeroes. Graph both functions on the same set of axes.

1. $x^2 + 1 = 2x$

   $y =$ _____

x	−1	0	1	2	3
y					

   _____

2. $4x − 2 = 2x^2$

   $y =$ _____

   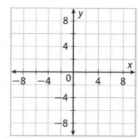

x	−1	0	1	2	3
y					

   _____

3. Can two different quadratic functions have the same zeroes? Explain.

   _____

   _____

Create a quadratic equation then solve the equation with a related function using a graphing calculator.

4. A skydiver jumps out of a plane 5,000 feet above the ground and her parachute opens 3,000 feet above the ground. A second skydiver jumps out of the same plane at the same time, but does not open his parachute until 2,000 feet above the ground. The function $h(t) = −16t^2 + 5,000$, where t represents the time in seconds, gives the height h, in feet, of the skydivers as they fall. How much longer does the second skydiver fall, neglecting air resistance? Round to the nearest tenth of a second.

   _____

5. An archway has vertical sides 10 feet high. The top of an archway can be modeled by the quadratic function $f(x) = −0.5x^2 + 10$ where x is the horizontal distance, in feet, along the archway. How far apart are the walls of the archway? Round your answer to the nearest tenth of a foot.

Name _____ Date _____ Class_____

LESSON 20-2

Connecting Intercepts and Linear Factors

Practice and Problem Solving: A/B

Graph each quadratic function and each of its linear factors. Then identify the x-intercepts and the axis of symmetry of each parabola.

1. $y = (x-1)(x-5)$

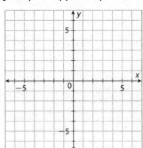

2. $y = (x-3)(x+2)$

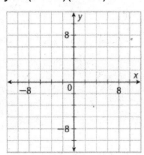

_____   _____

_____   _____

Write each function in standard form.

3. $y = 5(x+3)(x-2)$

4. $y = -2(x-3)(x-1)$

_____   _____

Graph the axis of symmetry, the vertex, the point containing the y-intercept, and another point. Then reflect the points across the axis of symmetry. Connect the points with a smooth curve.

5. $y = (x-1)(x+3)$

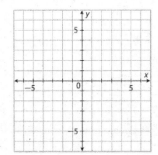

6. $y = (x+1)(x-3)$

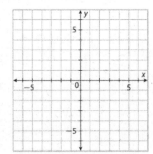

LESSON
20-2

Connecting Intercepts and Linear Factors
Practice and Problem Solving: C

Graph each quadratic function and each of its linear factors. Then identify the *x*-intercepts and the axis of symmetry of each parabola.

1. $y = 2(x-1)(x-5)$

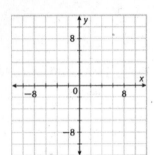

2. $y = -(x-3)(x+2)$

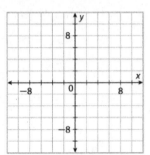

_____

_____

Write each function in standard form.

3. $y = (-3x-4)(2x-1)$

4. $y = \frac{2}{3}(3x-2)(3x+6)$

_____

_____

Graph the axis of symmetry, the vertex, the point containing the *y*-intercept, and another point. Then reflect the points across the axis of symmetry. Connect the points with a smooth curve.

5. $y = \frac{1}{2}(x-8)(x+2)$

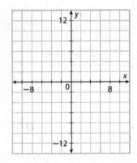

6. $y = (x+1)(x-3)$

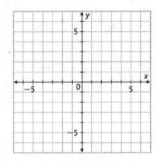

LESSON 20-3 Applying the Zero Product Property to Solve Equations

Practice and Problem Solving: A/B

Find the zeros of each function.

1. $f(x) = (x - 3)(x + 5)$

   _____

2. $f(x) = x(x - 1)$

   _____

3. $f(x) = (x + 1)(x + 1)$

   _____

4. $f(x) = (x - 5)(x + 1)$

   _____

5. $f(x) = x(x - 3)$

   _____

6. $f(x) = (x - 6)(x + 1)$

   _____

7. $f(x) = (x - 11)(x - 1)$

   _____

8. $f(x) = (x + 13)(x + 5)$

   _____

9. $f(x) = (x + 5)(x - 8)$

   _____

10. $f(x) = (x - 7)(x + 2)$

    _____

Use the Distributive Property and the Zero Product Property to solve the equations.

11. $f(x) = 2x(x - 2) + 14(x - 2)$

    _____

12. $f(x) = x(x - 4) - 2(x - 4)$

    _____

13. $f(x) = 5x(x - 3) + 25(x - 3)$

    _____

14. $f(x) = 3x(x - 7) + 7(x - 7)$

    _____

Solve.

15. The height of a javelin after it has left the hand of the thrower can be modeled by the function $h = 3(4t - 2)(-t + 4)$, where h is the height of the javelin and t is the time in seconds. How long is the javelin in the air?

    _____

16. The height of a flare fired from the deck of a ship can be modeled by $h = (-4t + 24)(4t + 4)$ where h is the height of the flare above water in feet and t is the time in seconds. Find the number of seconds it takes the flare to hit the water.

    _____

LESSON 20-3

Applying the Zero Product Property to Solve Equations
Practice and Problem Solving: C

Find the zeros of each function.

1. $f(x) = (3x - 1)(2x + 3)$

   _____

2. $f(x) = (x + 12)(x - 8)$

   _____

3. $f(x) = (x - 12)(x - 9)$

   _____

4. $f(x) = x(x - 1)(x - 1)$

   _____

5. $f(x) = (x + 6)(x - 5)$

   _____

6. $f(x) = (x - 3)(x + 2)$

   _____

7. $f(x) = (x + 9)(x - 2)$

   _____

8. $f(x) = (x - 1)(x - 1)$

   _____

9. $f(x) = (x - 1)(x + 1)(x + 2)(x - 2)$

   _____

10. $f(x) = 4(x + 7)(x - 1)$

    _____

Use the Distributive Property and the Zero Product Property to find the zeros of each function.

11. $f(x) = 2x(x + 3) - 4(x + 3)$

    _____

12. $f(x) = 3x(x + 7) - 2x - 14$

    _____

13. $f(x) = x^2 + 4x - 3(x + 4)$

    _____

14. $f(x) = 2x(x + 4) + 3x + 12$

    _____

Solve.

15. The height of an arrow after it has left the bow can be modeled by the function $h = 2t(3t - 9)$, where h is the height of the arrow and t is the time in seconds. How long is the arrow in the air before it hits the target?

    _____

16. The height of a person after he has left the trampoline in a jump can be modeled by the function $h = -3t(-4t + 8)$, where h is the height of the person and t is the time in seconds. How long is the person in the air before he lands back on the trampoline?

    _____

LESSON 21-1

Solving Equations by Factoring $x^2 + bx + c$

Practice and Problem Solving: A/B

What factors are shown by the algebra tiles?

1.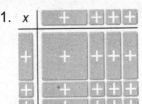

2.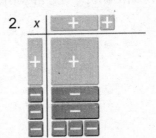

_____   _____

Factor.

3. $x^2 - 3x - 4$

4. $x^2 + 4x + 3$

5. $x^2 - 14x + 45$

_____   _____   _____

6. $x^2 + 11x + 24$

7. $x^2 - 12x + 32$

8. $x^2 - 15x + 36$

_____   _____   _____

9. $x^2 - 11x - 42$

10. $x^2 - 18x + 81$

11. $x^2 - 7x - 44$

_____   _____   _____

Solve by factoring.

12. $x^2 = 5x$

13. $x^2 = 9x - 18$

14. $x^2 - 15x + 50 = 0$

_____   _____   _____

15. $x^2 = -4x + 21$

16. $x^2 + 7x = 8$

17. $x^2 = -2x + 15$

_____   _____   _____

Solve.

18. The product of two consecutive integers is 72. Find all solutions.

_____

19. The length of a rectangle is 8 feet more than its width. The area of the rectangle is 84 square feet. Find its length and width.

_____

LESSON 21-1 Solving Equations by Factoring $x^2 + bx + c$

Practice and Problem Solving: C

What polynomials are shown by the algebra tiles?

1.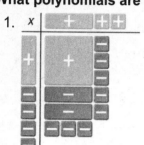

_____

2.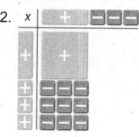

_____

3. A trinomial is in the form $x^2 + bx + c$, where $b < 0$ and $c > 0$. What do you know about the two factors?

_____

Solve by factoring.

4. $x^2 - 25 = 0$

_____

5. $x^2 - 2x + 1 = 0$

_____

6. $x^2 - 5x + 4 = 0$

_____

7. $x^2 - 9 + 2x + 1 = 0$

_____

8. $x^2 + x = 30$

_____

9. $x^2 = 36$

_____

10. $x + 3 = x^2 - 3$

_____

11. $x^2 + 3x - 11 = 43$

_____

12. $x^2 - 3x = 40$

_____

13. $x^2 = -3x + 28$

_____

14. $x^2 + 8x = -63 - 8x$

_____

15. $x^2 - 20 = x$

_____

Solve.

16. The product of two consecutive integers is five less than five times their sum. Find all possible solutions.

_____

17. The sum of the first n positive integers can be found using the formula $\dfrac{n(n + 1)}{2}$. How many integers must be added to get 253 as the sum?

_____

LESSON 21-2

Solving Equations by Factoring $ax^2 + bx + c$

Practice and Problem Solving: A/B

Solve the equations by factoring.

1. $2x^2 - 3x = 2x - 2$

_____

2. $3x^2 - 4x = 6x - 3$

_____

3. $3x^2 - 7x = x - 4$

_____

4. $5x^2 + 6x = -5x - 2$

_____

5. $4x^2 + 16x - 48 = 0$

_____

6. $2x^2 - 32 = 0$

_____

7. $2x^2 - 7 = 14 - 11x$

_____

8. $7x^2 - 12x = 36 + 7x$

_____

9. $5x^2 = 45$

_____

10. $2x^2 - 7x = 15 - 6x$

_____

11. $4x^2 - 20x = -25$

_____

12. $5x^2 - 20x + 20 = 0$

_____

13. $3x^2 + 5x = 6 - 2x$

_____

14. $2x^2 + 3x + 6 = 4x$

_____

15. $3x^2 = 9x$

_____

16. $9x^2 - 13x = 8x - 10$

_____

17. $4x^2 - 50x + 49 = 50x$

_____

18. $4x^2 + 21x = 6x - 14$

_____

19. $24x^2 - x = 10x - 1$

_____

20. $3x^2 + 12x - 15 = 0$

_____

Solve.

21. The height of a flare fired from the deck of a ship in distress can be modeled by $h = -16t^2 + 104t + 56$, where h is the height in feet of the flare above water and t is the time in seconds. Find the time it takes the flare to hit the water.

_____

Solving Equations by Factoring $ax^2 + bx + c$
Practice and Problem Solving: C

Simplify the equation. Then solve the equation by factoring.

1. $2x(x + 1) = 7x - 2$

_____

2. $3x(x - 2) = 4x - 3$

_____

3. $3x^2 = 4(2x - 1)$

_____

4. $5x(x + 1) = -2(3x + 1)$

_____

5. $4x(x + 4) = 48$

_____

6. $2(x + 3)(x - 3) = 14$

_____

7. $2x(x + 4) - 7 = 14 - 3x$

_____

8. $7x(x - 1) = 12(x + 3)$

_____

9. $8x^2 = 3(x^2 + 15)$

_____

10. $2x(x - 3) = 5(3 - x)$

_____

11. $2x(3x - 10) = 2x^2 - 25$

_____

12. $5x^2 - 2(x - 10) = 18x$

_____

13. $3x(x + 2) = 6 - x$

_____

14. $2x(x - 2) = -3(x - 2)$

_____

15. $0.3x^2 + x = 0.1x$

_____

16. $0.9x^2 - 1.3x = 0.8x - 1$

_____

17. $0.4x^2 - 5x + 4.9 = 5x$

_____

18. $1.5x^2 + 6x = 7.5$

_____

19. $6x^2 - \frac{7}{4}x = x - \frac{1}{4}$

_____

20. $8x^2 - \frac{2}{3}x = \frac{1}{3} + 7x^2$

_____

Solve.

21. The height of a ball thrown upward on the moon with a velocity of 8 meters per second can be modeled by $h = -0.8t^2 + 8t$, where h is the height of the ball in meters and t is the time in seconds. At what times will the height of the ball reach 19.2 meters?

_____

LESSON	**Using Special Factors to Solve Equations**
21-3	*Practice and Problem Solving: A/B*

Factor using the perfect-square technique.

1. $x^2 + 10xy + 25y^2$

2. $32x^2 + 80xy + 50y^2$

_____   _____

Factor using the difference of squares technique.

3. $81x^2 - 121y^2$

4. $75x^3 - 48x$

_____   _____

Solve each equation with special factors.

5. $50x^2 = 72$

6. $18x^3 + 48x^2 = -32x$

_____   _____

Solve.

7. A projectile is launched from a hole in the ground one foot deep. Its height follows the equation $h = -16t^2 + 8t - 1$. Use factoring by perfect-squares to find the time when the projectile lands back on the ground. (Hint: Landing on the ground means projectile height is zero.)

_____

8. Which of the following are solutions to $4x^3 - 16x = 0$?

   ○ A –2   ○ B –1   ○ C 0   ○ D 1   ○ E 2

LESSON 21-3

Using Special Factors to Solve Equations
Practice and Problem Solving: C

Factor using the perfect-square technique.

1. $27x^2 + 72xy + 48y^2$

2. $25x^3 - 60x^2y + 36xy^2$

_____   _____

Factor using the difference of squares technique.

3. $x^4 - 81$

4. $36x^4 - 16x^2y^2$

_____   _____

Solve each equation with special factors.

5. $-7x^3 + 100x = -75x$

6. $x^3 + 8x^2 + 4x = -x^3 - 4x$

_____   _____

Solve.

7. A projectile is launched from an underground silo 81 feet deep. Its height follows the equation $h = -16t^2 + 72t - 81$. Use factoring by perfect-squares to find the time when the projectile lands back on the ground.

_____

8. Which of the following are solutions to $81x^3 = 256x$?

   A $-\dfrac{16}{9}$ B $-\dfrac{4}{3}$ C 0   D $\dfrac{16}{9}$

Name _____ Date _____ Class_____

LESSON 22-1

Solving Equations by Taking Square Roots

Practice and Problem Solving: A/B

Solve. If the equation has no solution, give that as your answer.

1. $x^2 - 25 = 0$

_____

2. $x^2 + 25 = 0$

_____

3. $6x^2 - 6 = 0$

_____

4. $-3x^2 + 27 = 0$

_____

5. $-2x^2 - 1 = 0$

_____

6. $4x^2 - 100 = -100$

_____

7. $x^2 - 121 = 0$

_____

8. $x^2 - 49 = 0$

_____

9. $x^2 - 16 = 20$

_____

10. $(x+5)^2 - 6 = 43$

_____

11. $(x-1)^2 - 19 = 81$

_____

12. $(x-14)^2 + 13 = 14$

_____

13. $2(x-3)^2 + 1 = 73$

_____

14. $(x-1)^2 + 15 = 14$

_____

15. $-2(x+1)^2 - 5 = -55$

_____

Solve. Express square roots in simplest form.

16. $2(x+1)^2 - 1 = 9$

_____

17. $2(x-3)^2 + 7 = 19$

_____

18. $5(x-7)^2 + 10 = 25$

_____

Solve.

19. An auditorium has a floor area of 20,000 square feet. The length of the auditorium is twice its width. Find the dimensions of the room.

_____

20. A ball is dropped from a height of 64 feet. Its height, in feet, can be modeled by the function $h(t) = -16t^2 + 64$, where t is the time in seconds since the ball was dropped. After how many seconds will the ball hit the ground?

_____

21. A plot of land is in the shape of a square. The shaded square inside is covered with gravel. The rest of the square plot is covered in grass. Its area is 1400 square feet. How long are the sides of the square?

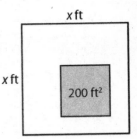

_____

LESSON 22-1

Solving Equations by Taking Square Roots

Practice and Problem Solving: C

1. Let $ax^2 + b = c$, where a, b, and c are real numbers and a is nonzero. How many real roots the equation has is determined by the relationship among a, b, and c. How are a, b, and c related if the equation has no real roots, one real root, or two real roots? Explain your reasoning.

_____

_____

_____

_____

2. Show, using the graph, that $0.5(x - 1)^2 + 3 = 0$ has no real roots. Then write an algebraic argument to support your conclusion.

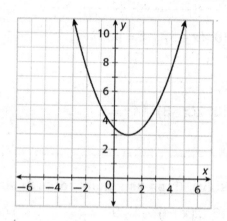

_____

_____

_____

_____

_____

_____

_____

3. Let $a(x - h)^2 = p$, where a, h, and p are positive real numbers. Show that this equation has two real roots. Then determine the sum of the roots. Explain your reasoning.

_____

_____

_____

_____

Solving Equations by Completing the Square
Practice and Problem Solving: A/B

Solve each equation by completing the square. The roots are integers.

1. $x^2 + 4x = 5$　　　　　　2. $x^2 - 2x = 8$　　　　　　3. $x^2 - 10x = -25$

　　_____　　　_____　　　_____

4. $x^2 + 2x = 15$　　　　　　5. $x^2 - 10x = 24$　　　　　6. $x^2 + 4x = 32$

　　_____　　　_____　　　_____

Solve each equation by completing the square. Express square roots in simplest form.

7. $x^2 - 2x = 1$　　　　　　8. $x^2 - 6x = -6$　　　　　9. $x^2 - 4x = -1$

　　_____　　　_____　　　_____

10. $2x^2 - 4x = 8$　　　　　11. $x^2 + 4x = -1$　　　　　12. $3x^2 - 12x = 3$

　　_____　　　_____　　　_____

13. $3x^2 - 6x = 21$　　　　　14. $3x^2 - 12x = 69$　　　　15. $5x^2 - 50x = -85$

　　_____　　　_____　　　_____

Solve.

16. A rectangular deck has an area of 320 ft². The length of the deck is
　　4 feet longer than the width. Find the dimensions of the deck. Solve by
　　completing the square.

　　_____

Solving Equations by Completing the Square
Practice and Problem Solving: C

Solve each problem.

1. For some real number b, the equation $x^2 + bx = -4$ has exactly one root. Determine that value of b and show your work.

_____
_____
_____
_____

2. The equation below is true for all real numbers x and only one real number b.

$$x^2 + 4x + 9 = (x + b)^2 + 5$$

Determine the value of b. Show your work.

_____
_____
_____
_____

3. Consider the function below.

$$y = x^2 - 6x + 14$$

For what value of x will $y = 5$? Determine this value of x and show your work.

_____
_____
_____

4. Let $y = x^2 + 4x - 21$. Use completing the square to show that the graph has two x-intercepts.
What are they? Show your work.

_____
_____
_____

LESSON 22-3 Using the Quadratic Formula to Solve Equations

Practice and Problem Solving: A/B

Solve using the quadratic formula.

1. $x^2 + x = 12$

2. $4x^2 - 17x - 15 = 0$

_____

_____

3. $2x^2 - 5x = 3$

4. $3x^2 + 11x + 5 = 0$

_____

_____

5. $x^2 - 11x + 28 = 0$

6. $x^2 - 49 = 0$

_____

_____

7. $6x^2 + x - 1 = 0$

8. $x^2 + 8x - 20 = 0$

_____

_____

Find the number of real solutions of each equation using the discriminant.

9. $x^2 + 25 = 0$

10. $3x^2 - x\sqrt{7} - 3 = 0$

11. $x^2 + 8x + 16 = 0$

_____ _____ _____

Solve.

12. In the past, professional baseball was played at the Astrodome in Houston, Texas. The Astrodome has a maximum height of 63.4 m. The height in meters of a baseball t seconds after it is hit straight up in the air with a velocity of 45 m/s is given by $h = -9.8t^2 + 45t + 1$. Will a baseball hit straight up with this velocity hit the roof of the Astrodome? Use the discriminant to explain your answer.

_____

_____

LESSON 22-3

Using the Quadratic Formula to Solve Equations

Practice and Problem Solving: C

Determine the number of real solutions for each equation. Then solve each equation that has one or more real solutions by using the quadratic formula.

1. $4x^2 + 7x = 10$

_____

2. $3x^2 - 4 = 4x$

_____

3. $2x^2 = 6x + 3$

_____

4. $14 - 3x^2 = 2x$

_____

5. $5x^2 + 4 = 3x + 2$

_____

6. $3x^2 - 12x = 8 - 15x$

_____

7. $3x^2 - 9 = 7x^2 - 12x$

_____

8. $9x^2 - 12x + 9 = 5x - 4x^2$

_____

9. $3x^2 + 9x + 5 = 1 - 2x^2$

_____

10. $7x^2 - 5x + 4 = 5x^2 - 2$

_____

11. $6x^2 - 49 + 34x = 6x + 10x^2$

_____

12. $9 - 8x^2 = 6x + 14$

_____

13. Explain what happens in the quadratic formula when there are no real roots for a quadratic equation.

_____

14. The length and width of a rectangular patio are $(x + 7)$ feet and $(x + 9)$ feet, respectively. If the area of the patio is 190 square feet, what are the dimensions of the patio?

_____

15. A model rocket is launched from a platform 12 meters high at a speed of 35 meters per second. Its height h can be modeled by the equation $h = -4.9t^2 + 35t + 12$, where t is the time in seconds. At what time will the rocket be at an altitude of 60 meters?

_____

LESSON 22-4	# Choosing a Method for Solving Quadratic Equations

Practice and Problem Solving: A/B

Solve each quadratic equation by any means. Identify the method and explain why you chose it. Express irrational answers in radical form and use a calculator to approximate your answer rounded to two decimal places.

1. $4x^2 = 64$

_____

_____

2. $4(x-3)^2 = 25$

_____

_____

3. $x^2 - 3x - 28 = 0$

_____

_____

4. $x^2 - x = 6$

_____

_____

5. $2x^2 - 4x - 3 = 0$

_____

_____

6. $x^2 + 10x - 3 = 0$

_____

_____

7. $1.5x^2 - 4.3x = -1.2$

_____

_____

8. $x^2 - \dfrac{1}{4} = 0$

_____

_____

Use any method to solve each quadratic equation. Identify the method and explain why you chose it. Convert irrational answers and fractions to decimals and round to the hundredths place.

9. The formula for height, in feet, of a projectile under the influence of gravity is given by $h = -16t^2 + vt + s$, where t is the time in seconds, v is the upward velocity at the start, and s is the starting height. Marvin throws a baseball straight up into the air at 70 feet per second. The ball leaves his hand at a height of 5 feet. When does the ball reach a height of 75 feet?

_____

_____

10. Use the projectile motion formula and solve the quadratic equation. Melissa drops a tennis ball from the roof of a building that is 256 feet high. How long does it take the tennis ball to hit the ground?

_____

_____

Choosing a Method for Solving Quadratic Equations
Practice and Problem Solving: C

Solve each quadratic equation by any means. Identify the method and explain why you chose it. Express irrational answers in radical form and use a calculator to approximate your answer rounded to two decimal places.

1. $\frac{1}{2}x^2 = \frac{1}{8}$

_____

_____

2. $2x^2 - 15x - 8 = 0$

_____

_____

3. $2\left(x + \frac{1}{2}\right)^2 = \frac{1}{2}$

_____

_____

4. $2x^2 + 7x - 15 = 0$

_____

_____

5. $3x^2 + 4x = 1$

_____

_____

6. $x^2 - 24x + 128 = 0$

_____

_____

7. $0.16x^2 + 0.08x + .01 = 0.16$

_____

_____

8. $0.36x^2 - 0.25 = 0$

_____

_____

Use any method to solve each quadratic equation. Identify the method and explain why you chose it. Convert irrational answers and fractions to decimals and round to the hundredths place.

9. The formula for height, in feet, of a projectile under the influence of gravity is given by $h = -16t^2 + vt + s$, where t is the time in seconds, v is the upward velocity at the start, and s is the starting height. Andrea launches a bottle rocket filled with water under pressure straight up into the air from the ground at a velocity of 48 feet per second. How long is the rocket in the air?

_____

_____

10. Use the projectile motion formula and solve the quadratic equation. Eric launches a water balloon straight up into the air from a platform five feet high at a velocity of 20 feet per second. Will the balloon hit the target suspended at a height of 50 feet? Explain how you know.

_____

_____

LESSON 22-5

Solving Nonlinear Systems

Practice and Problem Solving: A/B

Solve each system represented by the functions graphically.

1. $\begin{cases} y = x^2 - 2 \\ y = 5x - 8 \end{cases}$

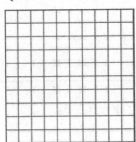

_____

2. $\begin{cases} y = x^2 - 4x + 6 \\ y = -x + 4 \end{cases}$

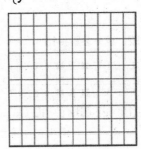

_____

Solve each system algebraically.

3. $\begin{cases} y = x^2 - 3 \\ y = -x + 3 \end{cases}$

_____

4. $\begin{cases} y = x^2 - 2x - 3 \\ y = -2x - 5 \end{cases}$

_____

5. $\begin{cases} y = 2x^2 + x - 3 \\ -3x + y = 1 \end{cases}$

_____

6. $\begin{cases} y = x^2 - 25 \\ y = x + 5 \end{cases}$

_____

7. $\begin{cases} y = x^2 - 1 \\ 2x - y = -2 \end{cases}$

_____

8. $\begin{cases} y = x^2 + 4x + 3 \\ x - y = -1 \end{cases}$

_____

Use a graphing calculator to solve.

9. A ball is thrown upward with an initial velocity of 40 feet per second from ground level. The height of the ball, in feet, after t seconds is given by $h = -16t^2 + 40t$. At the same time, a balloon is rising at a constant rate of 10 feet per second. Its height, in feet, after t seconds is given by $h = 10t$. Find the time it takes for the ball and the balloon to reach the same height.

_____

LESSON 22-5

Solving Nonlinear Systems

Practice and Problem Solving: C

Solve each system. If necessary, use the Quadratic Formula.

1. $y = x^2 + 13x - 46;\ y = 5x - 13$

2. $y = x^2 + 4;\ y = 2x - 9$

_____   _____

3. $y = 2x^2 + 7x + 12;\ y = 2x + 15$

4. $y = x^2 + 4x + 2;\ y = 1 - x$

_____   _____

5. $y = 4x^2 + 28x - 11;\ y = 3x + 10$

6. $y = 5x^2 + 9x + 7;\ y = 7 - 6x$

_____   _____

7. $y = 3x^2 - 4x - 1;\ y = -4x + 59$

8. $y = x^2 - 12x;\ y = -x^3$

_____   _____

9. $y = 2x^2 + 5x + 1;\ y = 3x^2 - x + 10$

10. $y = 15(x^2 + 2) - 19x;\ y = 15(x + 1)$

_____   _____

A ball is thrown directly upward from a height of h_0 feet with an initial velocity of v_0 feet per second. The ball's height after t seconds is given by the formula $h(t) = -16t^2 + v_0 t + h_0$. Use this information for Problems 11 and 12.

11. Suppose a ball is thrown directly upward from a height of 7 feet with an initial velocity of 50 feet per second. Use the Quadratic Formula or a graphing calculator to find the number of seconds it takes the ball to hit the ground. Round to the nearest tenth of a second.

_____

12. a. A helium balloon released from a height of h_0 feet rises at a constant rate of k feet per second. Its height after t seconds is given by the formula $h(t) = kt + h_0$. Suppose a helium balloon, released from a height of 25 feet at the same time as the ball in Problem 11, rises at 9 feet per second. After how many seconds will the ball and the balloon reach identical heights?

_____

   b. Examine your answer to Part a. Explain how it is physically possible for the ball and the balloon to have the same height twice.

_____

LESSON 23-1 **Modeling with Quadratic Functions**

Practice and Problem Solving: A/B

Determine if the function in the table is quadratic by finding the second differences. Write "is" or "is not". Justify your response.

1.

x	1	2	3	4	5	6
f(x)	−2	7	22	43	70	103

The function _____ a quadratic function.

_____

2.

x	1	2	3	4	5	6
f(x)	6	22	42	72	110	156

The function _____ a quadratic function.

_____

Each table can be represented by a quadratic function, $g(x) = ax^2 + bx + c$. Determine the values of a, b, and c to the nearest tenth. Write the equation for $g(x)$, the quadratic that is the best fit.

3.

x	1	2	3	4	5	6
f(x)	−3	9	29	57	93	137

a = _____ b = _____ c = _____ g(x) = _____

4.

x	1	2	3	4	5	6
f(x)	4	14	30	52	80	114

a = _____ b = _____ c = _____ g(x) = _____

5.

x	1	2	3	4	5	6
f(x)	7	12	24	37	55	77

a = _____ b = _____ c = _____ g(x) = _____

Solve.

6. The table represents plant height measured in inches over a six-week period. Write an equation for $g(x)$, the quadratic function that best fits the data. Round coefficients to the nearest tenth.

x	1	2	3	4	5	6
f(x)	1.4	2.4	3.8	5.4	7.4	10.1

LESSON 23-1	**Modeling with Quadratic Functions**

Practice and Problem Solving: C

1. The table below represents data that can be modeled by a quadratic equation, $g(x) = ax^2 + bx + c$.

x	1	2	3	4	5	6
f(x)	4.0	16.8	40.0	73.4	116.0	168.9

   a. Verify this by examining second differences.

   _____

   b. Find the values of a, b, and c, rounded to the nearest tenth, and write the equation.

   _____

   c. Consider the table of values below.

x	3	4	5	6	7	8
f(x)	4.0	16.8	40.0	73.4	116.0	168.9

   Without using a graphing calculator, find an equation for g', the quadratic model that is the best fit for this table. Explain.

   _____

   _____

2. The graph shown at the right can be modeled by a quadratic function.

   a. Verify by examining second differences.

   _____

   _____

   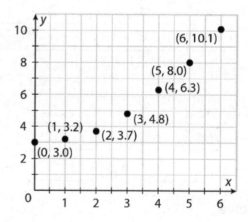

   b. Use a quadratic model to estimate y given $x = 2.5$. Show the work in obtaining the model and finding the estimate. Write the coefficients to the nearest tenth.

   _____

   _____

Comparing Linear, Quadratic, and Exponential Models

LESSON 23-2

Practice and Problem Solving: A/B

Complete the following to determine if each function is *linear*, *quadratic*, or *exponential*.

1. $f(x) = 2x + 1$

x	f(x)	1st difference	2nd difference	ratio
–2				
–1				
0				
1				
2				
3				

4. $f(x) = (x + 1)^2 - 3$

x	f(x)	1st difference	2nd difference	ratio
–2				
–1				
0				
1				
2				
3				

7. $f(x) = 3^x$

x	f(x)	1st difference	2nd difference	ratio
–2				
–1				
0				
1				
2				
3				

2. End behavior as *x* increases:

   $f(x)$ _____

3. $f(x)$ is: _____

5. End behavior as *x* increases:

   $f(x)$ _____

6. $f(x)$ is: _____

8. End behavior as *x* decreases:

   $f(x)$ _____

9. $f(x)$ is: _____

Use the following information for 10–11.

Todd had a piggy bank holding $384. He began taking out money each month. The table shows the amount remaining, in dollars, after each of the first four months.

Month	0	1	2	3	4
Amount	384	192	96	48	24

10. Does the data follow a linear, quadratic, or exponential model? How can you tell?

    _____

    _____

11. How much will be left in the piggy bank at the end of the fifth month?

    _____

Name _____ Date _____ Class_____

LESSON 23-2 Comparing Linear, Quadratic, and Exponential Models
Practice and Problem Solving: C

Complete the following to determine if each function is *linear*, *quadratic*, or *exponential*.

1. $f(x) = -10x + 1$

x	f(x)	1st difference	2nd difference	ratio
-1				
0				
1				
2				
3				
4				

4. $f(x) = 5x + 4 - x^2$

x	f(x)	1st difference	2nd difference	ratio
-1				
0				
1				
2				
3				
4				

7. $f(x) = 10^x + 1$

x	f(x)	1st difference	2nd difference	ratio
-1				
0				
1				
2				
3				
4				

2. End behavior as x increases:

   $f(x)$ _____

3. $f(x)$ is: _____

5. End behavior as x increases:

   $f(x)$ _____

6. $f(x)$ is: _____

8. End behavior as x decreases:

   $f(x)$ _____

9. $f(x)$ is: _____

Solve.

10. The functions $f(x) = x^2$ and $g(x) = 2^x$ both approach infinity as x approaches infinity. Write the function $h(x) = f(x) - g(x)$. Then determine the end behavior of $h(x)$ as x approaches infinity.

_____

11. An exponential function approaches 10 as x approaches infinity. Write a possible equation for the function.

_____

12. A function's second differences are constant but not 0. Can you conclude whether the function is exponential, linear, or quadratic?

_____

LESSON
24-1

Graphing Polynomial Functions

Practice and Problem Solving: A/B

Identify whether the polynomial $f(x)$ is of odd or even degree and whether the leading coefficient is positive or negative.

1.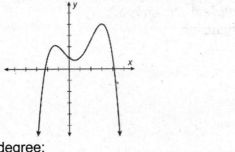

   degree: _____

   leading coefficient: _____

2.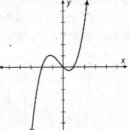

   degree: _____

   leading coefficient: _____

Identify each function as odd, even, or neither, and whether the leading coefficient is positive or negative.

3.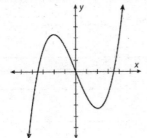

   function type: _____

   leading coefficient: _____

4.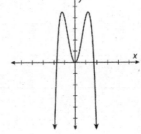

   function type: _____

   leading coefficient: _____

Identify:

- **the degree of the function**
- **whether the function is even, odd, or neither**
- **whether the leading coefficient is positive or negative**

5.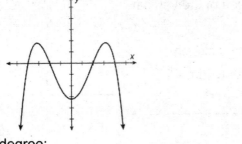

   degree: _____

   function type: _____

   leading coefficient: _____

6.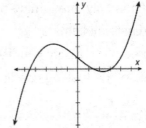

   degree: _____

   function type: _____

   leading coefficient: _____

Name _____ Date _____ Class_____

LESSON 24-1
Graphing Polynomial Functions
Practice and Problem Solving: C

Answer the following questions.

1. Only one of these graphs represents a polynomial function of degree 4,
   is an even function, and has a positive leading coefficient. Which is it?
   Explain why the other graphs do not represent the function.

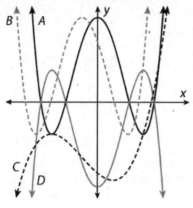

_____

_____

_____

_____

2. Show, by using the definition of an even function, that $f(x) = 2x^4 - 3x$ is
   not an even function.

_____

_____

3. Polynomial function f is defined by the following facts.
   - f is defined for all real numbers.
   - f is an odd function.
   - The graph of f has only one turning point to the left of the vertical
     axis in a coordinate system.

   What is the degree of f? Justify your response with a sketch.

   What can be said of the leading coefficient of the polynomial?

   _____

   _____

   _____

LESSON 24-2

Understanding Inverse Functions

Practice and Problem Solving: A/B

Graph the relation and connect the points. Then create an inverse table and graph the inverse. Identify the domain and range of each relation.

1.

x	–3	–2	–1	0	1
y	–1	1	3	5	7

Domain _____, Range _____

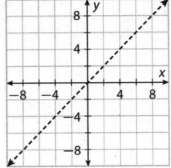

x					
y					

Domain _____, Range _____

2.

x	–2	–1	0	1	2
y	0	1	4	5	7

Domain _____, Range _____

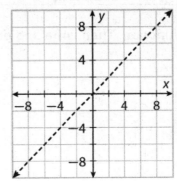

x					
y					

Domain _____, Range _____

Use inverse operations to find each inverse. Use a sample input for *x* to check.

3. $f(x) = 3x + 2$

_____

_____

4. $f(x) = \dfrac{2x}{5} - 3$

_____

_____

Graph each function. Then write and graph each function's inverse.

5. $f(x) = \dfrac{x}{3} + 3$ _____

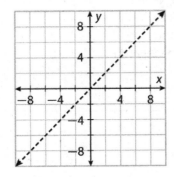

6. $f(x) = \dfrac{-x}{2} - 2$ _____

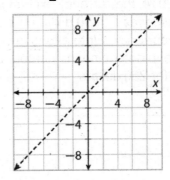

Name _____ Date _____ Class _____

Understanding Inverse Functions
Practice and Problem Solving: C

Use inverse operations to find each inverse. Check your solution with a sample input.

1. $f(x) = \dfrac{4x+3}{3}$

2. $f(x) = \dfrac{3x}{5} - 6$

_____   _____

_____   _____

Graph each function. Then write and graph each function's inverse.

3. $f(x) = \dfrac{2x}{5} + 2$

4. $f(x) = \dfrac{-3x}{4} - 3$

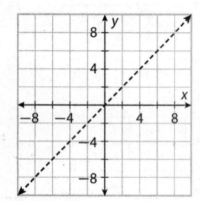   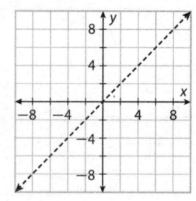

_____   _____

Solve.

5. Sandy wants to know how many miles he drove on the interstate toll road. The charge to enter the toll road is $4, and the per-mile rate is $0.13. The total charge when he exited the toll road was $35.20. Write a function to model the situation, and use the inverse to find the number of miles he drove. Make sure to check your answer.

_____

6. In March 2014, the currency exchange rate between the U.S. dollar and the Euro was 1.3858 dollars per Euro, plus a 5 dollar fee to exchange currency. Write a function to model the situation, and use the inverse to determine the number of Euros that would be received in exchange for 250 dollars.

_____

LESSON 24-3

Graphing Square Root Functions

Practice and Problem Solving: A/B

Identify the translation of the parent function. Tell whether each is a stretch or compression, and give the factor if applicable. Then find the domain of each function.

1. $y = \sqrt{x - 6}$

   _____

   _____

2. $y = 10\sqrt{x - 9}$

   _____

   _____

3. $y = \sqrt{1 - x}$

   _____

   _____

4. $y = \frac{1}{2}\sqrt{x - 2}$

   _____

   _____

Graph each square root function.

5. $y = \sqrt{x - 2}$

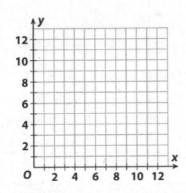

6. $y = 3\sqrt{x + 4} + 2$

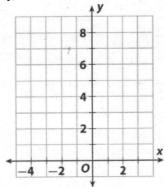

The function $d = 4.9t^2$ gives the distance, d, in meters, that an object dropped from a height will fall in t seconds. Use this for Problems 9–10.

7. Express t as a function of d.

   _____

8. Find the number of seconds it takes an object to fall 100 feet. Round to the nearest tenth of a second.

   _____

Name _____ Date _____ Class_____

Graphing Square Root Functions

Practice and Problem Solving: C

Find the domain of each function.

1. $y = 3 - \sqrt{x+3}$

2. $y = \frac{2}{5}\sqrt{3-x}$

_____

_____

3. $y = \frac{1}{4}\sqrt{x-9} - 3$

4. $y = 2\sqrt{x} + 3\sqrt{x-1}$

_____

_____

Graph each square root function. Then describe the graph as a transformation of the graph of the parent function $y = \sqrt{x}$, and give its domain and range.

5. $y = 10 - 4\sqrt{x-1}$

6. $y = 1 + \sqrt{2x+9}$

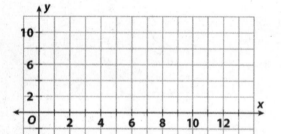

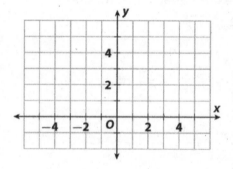

_____

_____

_____

_____

_____

_____

Solve.

7. The relation $y^2 = x$ is not a function. Explain why. Then write the relation as two functions that can be graphed together on a graphing calculator to represent the original relation.

_____

_____

8. Examine the function $f(x) = \sqrt{x+4} - \sqrt{x}$ on a graphing calculator. Explain why its range is all positive numbers less than or equal to 2.

_____

_____

Graphing Cube Root Functions

LESSON 24-4

Practice and Problem Solving: A/B

Find the inverse of each cubic function.

1. $f(x) = x^3$

   _____

2. $f(x) = \dfrac{1}{8}x^3$

   _____

3. $f(x) = -27x^3$

   _____

4. $f(x) = 5x^3$

   _____

5. $f(x) = 125x^3 - 7$

   _____

6. $f(x) = x^3 + 8$

   _____

Graph the cube root function.

7. $y = \sqrt[3]{2x}$

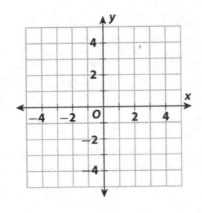

8. $y = \sqrt[3]{-\dfrac{x}{3}}$

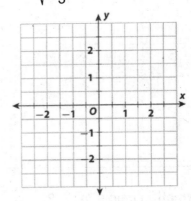

In a square cylinder, height, h, equals diameter, d. The function

$V = \dfrac{\pi}{4}d^3$ **gives the volume, V, of a square cylinder. Use this for 9–10.**

9. Express d as a function of V.

   _____

10. Find the diameter of a square cylinder with a volume of 300 cubic inches. Round to the nearest tenth of an inch.

    _____

LESSON 24-4

Graphing Cube Root Functions

Practice and Problem Solving: C

Find the inverse of each cubic function.

1. $f(x) = 8x^3 - 1$

2. $f(x) = (x + 3)^3 + 2$

_____   _____

3. $f(x) = -\dfrac{1}{1000}x^3 + 27$

4. $f(x) = 6 - 5(x - 1)^3$

_____   _____

Write the equation of the cube root function whose graph is shown.

5.

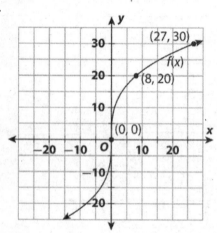

6.

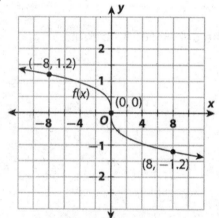

_____   _____

Use the information below for 7–9.

According to the Third Law of Johannes Kepler (1571–1630), the square of the orbital period of a planet is proportional to the cube of its distance from the Sun. This is expressed in the formula $T^2 = a^3$, where T is measured in years and a is measured in astronomical units (1 astronomical unit is the mean distance of Earth from the Sun).

7. Express T as a function of a. Express a as a function of T.

_____

8. Mercury's mean distance from the Sun is approximately 38.7% that of Earth's. Estimate Mercury's orbital period. Show your work.

_____

9. Jupiter's orbital period is approximately 11.9 times that of Earth's. Estimate Jupiter's mean distance from the Sun. Show your work.

_____